WALKING WITH THE WAVES

A JOURNEY ON THE SOUTH WEST COAST PATH

WALKING WITH THE WAVES

COPYRIGHT © 2022 ROBERT ELLIOTT

ALL RIGHTS RESERVED. NO REPRODUCTION WITHOUT WRITTEN PERMISSION.

WWW.ROBBYE64@HOTMAIL.COM

ISBN: 9798795948812

CONTENTS:

PREFACE..5

DORSET..11

SOUTH DEVON..45

CORNWALL...109

NORTH DEVON & SOMERSET......................199

WITH THANKS..235

4

PREFACE

In 2014, while scrolling through the countless online videos of people hiking long distance trails all over the world, I found one that fascinated me. It was filmed as a documentary with in-depth analysis of all aspects of the trail; daily life, re-supplying in towns, the weather, flora and fauna and geological wonders that excited me to my very core. From that moment on, the term 'Thru-hike' was something that would be etched into my soul and something that I would crave. The Pacific Crest Trail* was soon to be an ambition beyond any I'd encountered before, and inspire a complete change within me.

The logistics of undertaking such a lengthy journey of 2,653 miles in another country was daunting at first, but soon there was a realisation that other people, from all over the globe, were following the same dream as I, and the more I learned about the trail, the more comfortable I felt, and the more solid the ambition became.

Financially, I wasn't in any kind of position to follow the goal, and so I set a date, to save as much money as possible by the spring of 2018, so that I may step foot upon the trail in april of that year. In the meantime, I would buy new equipment and clothing, train in the mountains and on local paths and prepare my body for what would most certainly be the greatest physical and emotional challenge of my life, living for six months in the North American wilderness.

All was going according to plan and by february 2017, finances were looking good, and I had purchased a lot of the gear I would be taking with me. Unfortunately, this was all set to change and due to personal circumstances, my life took a completely different direction soon after.

The dream would always burn inside me but events in my life had pulled me away, and eventually the ambition stalled completely. It wasn't until the spring of 2018 that my lifes' direction had changed once again, and the aspirations I'd felt a year earlier had thankfully returned. This time, I vowed that nothing was going to stop me.

A new date was set. Two more years of work to save up more money, and I would be setting off for the California/Mexico border to begin the trip of a lifetime. 2020 was going to be the year that changed me forever, when I'd see wonderous sights and meet incredible people. The year that I would challenge myself beyond anything I'd accomplished before, the year my dream would finally become a reality.

The year 2020....a miserable year for many people. A year in which a global pandemic had swept across every country around the world. A time of restrictions upon movement by governments, a time of uncertainty, job losses, business closures, fear and panic in the community....and people dying, many people dying. For weeks in the spring of 2020, the UK had imposed total lockdowns across the nation, warning people to stay at home, and by the summer, had made it mandatory to wear face masks in public places. The freedom that I'd been craving for the past six years, was taken away from me, from everybody, in only a matter of weeks.

With my flight cancelled just five weeks before I was due to travel, I felt like the carpet had been pulled from under my feet. I was devastated. Only weeks before, I was watching videos of the Pacific Crest Trail and thinking 'i'll soon be there, living the dream'.

I'd applied for a sabbatical from work to cover the time I had planned to spend in the USA, but being unable to go, I was forced to cancel it and return to work, to the mundane life I was trying so hard to escape. A couple of months passed by, and there was still a burning inside of me to find some freedom within this crazy, restricted lifestyle we were all living in. When certain restrictions within the country were eventually lifted, it provided an opportunity for limited travel, to go hiking and camping, to explore nature once again. It was during this period that I made a huge decision. If I couldn't do a thru-hike in another country, I would do one in the UK.

The longest trail is the South West Coast Path, which snakes its way along the coasts of Dorset, Devon, Cornwall and Somerset for 630 miles. I'd always been keen to do this one day and so I decided now was the perfect time. This would mean re-applying for my sabbatical, as the trail would take me over a month to complete, but it really wasn't an issue for me. I had enough money saved and having planned on taking the time off work anyway, the only difference would be what I *did* with that time.

The biggest decision to make was my living arrangements, but on august 10th 2020, on a very hot summer morning, I posted the keys through the letterbox of my cosy one-bedroomed flat, set in a quiet, rural village, and changed my life once again. Over the coming month or so, I'd be living out of my tent, eating food from a camp stove, walking many miles each day over some incredibly rough terrain, catching ferries across wide estuaries, seeing new places, meeting new people, watching the sun rise and set across the ocean and most important of all, I'd finally feel free.

The Pacific Crest Trail is 2,653 miles long, beginning at the Mexican border near Campo, California and terminating near Manning Park, Canada. It passes through the states of California, Oregon and Washington and crosses ten mountain ranges. Its highest point is Forester Pass at 13,153ft and its lowest point is Cascade Locks on the Oregon/Washington border at 140ft. Every year, hundreds of hopeful hikers from across the globe attempt the arduous five month trek, through some of the most glorious scenery to be found anywhere in the world.

DORSET

AUGUST 12TH

It was blisteringly hot when I arrived in Poole to drop off my rental car. I was still a few miles from the official start of the trail at South Haven Point, and rather than endure an agonising road walk along traffic-laden streets in baking sunshine, I asked the guys behind the rental counter if they would book a taxi for me. I stood with my incredibly heavy backpack in the midday sun, waiting to be taken to Sandbanks, where I would catch the ferry across Poole harbour and my journey would begin, but it was apparent, after at least a half hour wait, that my transport was not coming.

"What a great start to the journey", I snarled to myself, while wiping beads of sweat from my burning forehead.

The guy that I'd handed my keys to on my arrival was still milling around the gravelled car park, checking other vehicles that had been recently returned and we eventually caught eye contact.

"Has your taxi not turned up yet?" he enquired in a playful tone.

I felt my eyes beginning to roll at the clearly obvious retort that I would have to sputter. "Err...no!" I remarked, as sarcastically as I could without offending him. "Is there any chance you could make another call for me?"

He darted inside swiftly and I peered around the door to the rental counter, watching his every move to make sure he picked up the phone. He glanced at me several times as he spoke to the taxi firm (clearly for the first time, and not a follow-up call as he had led me to believe) and finally muttered "All sorted".

I gave him a simple thumbs up and headed back into the heat.

Another sweltering twenty minutes passed before a car entered the rental compound at lightning speed and skidded on the shale in front of me. A friendly face wound down the window and revealed he was there to give me a ride to the ferry. With much relief, I threw my pack onto the rear seat and climbed into a comfy air-conditioned vehicle.

It was a pleasant drive, passing through Poole town centre and along the Sandbanks seafront and the very expensive houses that lined the harbour. The taxi driver, though clearly not from the UK, was very chatty and incredibly knowledgeable about the local area and expressed great interest in my upcoming thru-hike. It was a welcome change from annoyance of the previous hour and I was feeling much calmer by the end of the short journey.

I couldn't have timed my arrival at the ferry point better. There was a long queue of vehicles waiting to board, many of them with windows wide open in the searing heat, and my stroll to the foot passenger waiting area was an audible melee of eclectic music genres, thumping heavy drum beats and booming basslines. I found it quite difficult to not walk in time with the steady rhythm's blaring from each vehicle I passed, and I became very self-conscious when I noticed people watching me. The more I tried to step *out* of time, the more awkward my gait became, so I was relieved to reach the standing passenger queue, and even happier to be allowed to board the ferry and take a seat. Even while sitting, I still found myself foot-tapping to the music as the myriad of cars were ushered onto the deck.

It was quite a while before all vehicles were loaded, giving me plenty of time to soak up the spectacular views across Poole Harbour to the bustling South Haven Point, where my journey would begin imminently.

After only a brief and windy crossing, the ferry halted against the opposite shore and I gawked at the beach through squinted eyes, through a haze of shimmering sunbeams and pure radiance. The reality of what was to come finally hit me. I thought briefly about the miles and the adventure that lay before me. It was quite an over-whelming thought, but one that filled me with intrigue and excitement. "This is it", I pondered for a second, and as the multitude of vehicles noisely disembarked the ferry and continued on their journey behind me, I took that first step into the unknown.

It wasn't long before i arrived at the trail start/end sign. A wonderful blue painted metal structure with dolphins, deer and sea birds carved into it. I took my first photo and looked at the clock. 12:18pm wednesday, august 12th. Setting the pedometer running on my phone I began to walk. To where, I wasn't entirely sure. I couldn't see another sign ahead of me and the map on my phone didn't give an exact direction. Instead I saw endless sand dunes and a haze of beach dwellers enjoying the cloudless summer skies. Some lay motionless, baking their already tanned bodies, while others cooled off in the blue-green lapping waves. Yes, this was the direction i needed to walk and I reluctantly trudged through soft sand and marram grass, with no end in sight.

It wasn't the best start to a long hike, i'll be honest. After only twenty minutes my calves were burning. It felt like i'd run a marathon in a huge rabbit costume and my shoulders ached from the intense weight as the straps on my pack etched their way through my boney clavicle. My back was pooling sweat due to the incessant heat and my forehead was already starting to redden. There was no shelter to be had anywhere. It was a horrible experience and if i'd have been out for a day hike, i'd have probably turned around and gone home. I told myself to 'just get my head down and get through this', knowing it wasn't going to last forever. What I neglected to tell myself, was that it could get worse.

Imagine my shock when I was faced with three naked middle-aged men, hands on hips, standing proudly atop the dunes looking in my direction. I knew there was a nudist beach along that stretch of coast, it says it clearly on the maps, but nothing can prepare you for the reality. I thought I had wisely ventured off the main trail a sufficient distance to avoid this kind of interaction, but alas, it wasn't far enough. Averting my own eyes downward, but still sensing the gaze from three pairs of eyes above me, I quickened my pace. My calves didn't thank me for this, but every other molecule of me did.

After 3.8 miles of sand dunes, i finally hit a paved road. It was such a relief to be walking normally again on solid ground. There were many people milling about, carrying collapsible sun beds and rubber rings. Lines of burned shoulders queued for over-priced ice cream and the stench of barbeque fluid drifted from the car park beyond, where families gorged on burgers from the boot of their vehicles. The smell made me realise how hungry I was, so I decided that when i came across the next suitable place for a break, I would take my pack off and have lunch. It wasn't quite as tasty as the burgers had smelt, but a few energy bars and plenty of electrolyte-filled water was very welcomed by my groaning stomach and I sat for a good twenty minutes looking across Studland Bay, to the coast I would be walking upon soon, and to Old Harry Rocks. It was the first point of interest i'd marked and the first place I knew I would recognise from the online videos I'd previously watched. My first milestone was upon me.

As I hoisted my heavy pack onto my shoulders once again, I turned to see a figure walking towards me. It was most definitely another hiker, I could see his pack clinging to his shoulders like a small child. He was heading in the opposite direction to me, so it took me by surprise when, rather than just saying hello, he asked if he was on the right track to Swanage. After introductions, Noel informed me he had taken the bus from Poole and had intended to start the trail where I had, but instead of getting off the bus at the ferry terminal, he'd continued on until it had taken him five miles further than he had expected. In some ways I'm a little annoyed that I didn't do that myself after the hell I'd put myself through walking along the beach, but if we'd have both executed our plans differently, then we would never have met, and I'm thankful we did.

We hiked together for the rest of the day, entering the small town of Swanage during the sweltering late afternoon heat and deciding to partake in a couple of well earned cold beers. This was not something I would have done myself after only a few hours on trail, but we spent a pleasant hour or two discussing many topics, and putting the world to rights. Before continuing on the trail to find camp, we headed back into the village centre for extra food and a few more beers. It had been such a relaxing afternoon, the idea of ending the day with a stunning sunset and a couple of tinnies sounded very appealing, despite the extra weight.

As the dazzling sun began to melt into the western skyline, we were thankfully at a point on the trail with plenty of camping options. We chose a grassy bank next to a stone wall, set back about a hundred yards from the trail. It wasn't the flattest ground, but it was soft, relatively sheltered and had a great sea view, something I'd been looking forward to all day. Noel had told me earlier of his brand new, never-before-pitched two person tent. Having plenty of experience with such matters, I offered my services to help him out and with a few tweaks to the guy ropes and pegs, we managed to erect it successfully within fifteen minutes. Mine within five. It was then food time, and the enjoyment of the extra beers we'd packed out, while gazing out to sea and the first glorious sunset of the trip.

AUGUST 13TH

I didn't wake particularly early the next morning. Hiking with another person had changed things for me. Usually, i'd have been up at the crack of dawn and i'd have done six miles before 9am, but there seemed to be less urgency now. I strolled down the gentle slope to where we had pitched Noel's tent. He was already up and didn't look quite as refreshed as i felt. He'd not slept well at all due to the cold, which I thought was quite strange as I'd been very warm and slept like a baby. It later transpired that Noel had dismissed the idea of packing a sleeping bag for his trip due to it being the height of summer and he had expected warm nights. It was instantly obvious that he hadn't spent too many nights camping by the sea before. To top off his faux pas, he had also forgotten to zip up the fly on his new tent, leaving only a thin mesh between him and the elements. It was no wonder he was cold and it was no major surprise to hear his decision to head back towards Swanage to buy himself a sleeping bag. I couldn't wait around for him and I certainly didn't want to walk back those extra miles, so we exchanged phone numbers and agreed the best course of action would be to meet up further along the trail in a few days time, possibly at Weymouth. We said our goodbyes and I prepared, once more, to hit the trail alone. I got a text from Noel later in the day to say that he had jumped on a train and was heading home. We never did meet again.

I pushed onward towards Kimmeridge Bay. The weather was set fair and a good six degrees cooler than the day before. It really was quite a pleasant day to be hiking next to the sea. So nice in fact, i wore my shorts for the first time. I'd refrained from wearing them the day before, not only because it was probably too hot and I didnt want to get sunburned legs on the first day, but probably more so, the fact i'd have dazzled everyone in Swanage with my pure white skin, which seemed to reflect the sunlight with utmost intensity. I burned them on day two instead!

Day two brought the first serious climbs of the trip, some of which seemed to be vertical, so I spent a lot of time admiring the stunning views from each crest i summited, even if it *was* primarily to get my breath back. It's always a bonus when reaching the top of a big climb, to find a perfectly positioned bench on which to regain the strength in ones legs (and breathe normally again) and I took full advantage...of them all. I was still making good mileage despite the amount of breaks I was taking and it wasn't too long before I was nearing the Lulworth Ranges, an area i'd hiked before and an area I knew was off limits to walkers at certain times of the year due to military activity.

I had no idea whether i'd be able to continue on the main trail or not, so I was more than grateful to see the signs upon an open gate, knowing I wouldn't have to add mileage to my day with a lengthy diversion. Although it was a shorter route, the main trail through the ranges was quite arduous in places. Long gravel tracks built for military vehicles took their toll on my calves and ankles and the steep climbs and descents of the day were felt in my tiring knees.

As I headed towards the towering chalk hill of Hambury Tout, there was hope in sight for a slightly more forgiving trail, if only i could find it. I'd managed to divert off the main trail without realising it and ended up on a hill with a few wild ponies and just a view of where I needed to be. I sat down to consult the map and find out where i'd gone wrong. While I'd stopped I opted to put my hiking trousers back on, as the afternoon sun was slowly disappearing behind looming clouds on the horizon and the first chill of evening was blowing across the pasture ahead of me. I should have taken a look around before removing my shorts though. As I sat in my underwear rummaging through my pack for the change of legwear, I was passed by a rather attractive lady out running. She smiled and continued on her way. My embarrassment would have been spared were it not for the fact we would meet again shortly after, as we both searched for the trail. Confused about which direction we should be heading to connect with the right path, our own paths crossed several times until finally she disappeared over the brow of a hill and out of sight. It was then I realised she must have found her way, and so I followed.

The path indeed steered me into the tiny village of West Lulworth and back to the coast path. As i approached a large car park near an ice cream stall, my eyes met with the lovely running lady once again. She smiled as she saw me and I walked over to her, laughing about my map reading incompetence. Talking to her properly for the first time, I realised she was from the north and had the sweetest voice I'd heard in a long time. She'd been stressing as much as I had about finding the correct path, as her bus was leaving very shortly, so we didn't talk for long, but that may have been due to my own inevitable short-comings about conversing with pretty women, rather than a public transport timetable. I wished her a good evening and turned to face the steep climb up to Hambury Tout, looking back after several steps, just for one more glimpse of that beautiful blonde hair, glinting in the late afternoon sun, but she had already moved on. It's safe to say I'll never see her lovely face again, but it's a moment I will always be fond of.

I reached Lulworth Cove with a nineteen mile day under my belt. I didn't actually see the impressive rock formation of Durdle Door though. The main trail runs directly past it, but there were so many people around that I opted for an alternative route that took me through a holiday park full of caravans, a small coppice with signs warning me of snakes and onto an open field full of cows.... and possibly more snakes too. The day was reaching its conclusion and the rain was fast approaching from the west, so I made a decision to cut inland to find a camp spot. It was a gamble, but I took a side trail and climbed a modest 125 metres from sea level to the brow of a hill, which overlooked the humorously named valley 'Scratchy Bottom'. There were a couple of trails running in different directions from that point, but with the dusk approaching and my weary legs telling me I shouldn't proceed any further, I picked a sheltered spot behind a hawthorn hedgerow and sat for a few minutes, surveying the area.

There were cows in all directions, but they were some distance away. With plenty of reminders that cows had been in the vicinity recently (if you know what I mean) I pondered on the validity of my location choice, wondering if they would return at some point during the night to leave me more reminders that this was their land and frighten the hell out of me at 2am. I decided to take my chances and began to pitch my tent.

After eating a hearty dehydrated meal, an oxymoron if ever there was one, I nestled down in my cosy sleeping bag for a good nights sleep, but it wasn't long before I was awoken rather suddenly in an eerie half light by the sound of voices. One male, one female. I froze completely, listening intently to pinpoint their direction and heading. Late night walkers I presumed, but one can never be too sure. Their voices floated across the hill top in the stiff breeze, leaving me uncertain as to their exact location. At one moment they sounded so close, then seemed to drift away. It wasn't until a dog barked that I became fully alert. The dog was most definitely closer than the people and possibly only several yards from me. I began to panic a little, wondering if they were landowners scouting the area, and I was preparing myself for a torch light on my tent and a stern voice telling me to move on, but it never came, the dog bark was the very last sound I heard for the rest of the night. It was almost like they'd disappeared. It was very strange, but I welcomed the silence. I drifted into slumber soon after and awoke at the crack of dawn to a beautiful misty sunrise and calming birdsong. I was fully refreshed.

AUGUST 14TH

It was day three and my intentions were firmly fixed on covering as great a distance as possible now that my legs had recovered from the endless climbs of the previous day. I could see the coast path a couple of hundred yards away as I stretched in the morning sun. I took a parallel trail which was hardly used and the grass was long and very damp, but I knew it would eventually join with the main path, just before a large obelisk overlooking the sea, according to the map. The pyramid stone structure must have been some kind of navigation beacon, but with no inscription I could see, I admired its majesty only for a brief moment before pushing on.

The grasslands before me were comforting. An inviting shade of ochre, doused in glittering morning dew. They seemed to be thankful and refreshed after the preceding days heat and bowed their heads under the weight of each water droplet. I felt privileged to be sharing the earth with them. There was an overwhelming sense of calm and my first true feeling of being at one with nature. To the south, the sea caressed the cliff bottoms and gulls soared effortlessly over the pinnacles. The trail itself was uncomplicated. Smooth, sturdy clay, hardened by the hot summer days made walking easy and i descended steadily towards the wooded village of Ringstead with a calming smile on my face. It was there where I encountered the first person of the day. A dog walker. He may have thought it strange when he approached me, as I collected water from a shallow stream under a stone bridge. A simple nod of the head from us both was all that was needed. Even his dog seemed disinterested as I filtered about a litre and a half into plastic bottles, loaded up my pack and set off towards Osmington Mills.

The next few miles brought new challenges. I had originally planned on staying at a camp site at Osmington Mills, but as I approached the area it became instantly clear that that would have been almost impossible.

Being in the midst of a global pandemic when people were unable to travel abroad for their summer holidays as they would normally, meant they had chosen to spend their vacation in the UK instead, and if I hadn't have known better, would have assumed they had all decided to head to this very campsite. It was rammed with tents, caravans and motorhomes. There was so little space on the site that some tents even spilled onto the trail itself, blocking my path and forcing me to walk between the hordes of holidaymakers in a sea of canvas and stripey windbreakers. This was glamping at its finest. Oversized cooking stoves laden with sizzling bacon and sausages cast a smokey haze onto the morning breeze and followed me alluringly. A cacophony of whistling kettles and not-so-portable radios competed for every cubed inch of silent morning air. Children, removed from their daily routines of television and computer games, chased one another through the maze of guy ropes and parked vehicles. Dogs, generators and a constant murmur of indistinct voices from every direction seemed to envelop me. I have never understood why people enjoy that kind of holiday and I probably never will. It was like I was walking through a housing estate, although in lieu of solid brick, there were flimsy canvas walls with clear plastic windows. I felt eyes upon me as I exited the campsite as swiftly as my legs could carry me.

After relentless heat and humidity of the previous couple of days, I became aware of the grime and sweat that clung to my clothes and I was starting to smell a little, well, a lot actually. It's a distinctive smell that I've never gotten used to, despite the amount of multi-day hiking I had done previously and after a while, I started to get paranoid with each person that I passed on the trail. It was something that I was going to have to address as soon as possible and I considered my options.

Proceeding at my current pace would keep me in the Weymouth vicinity and so I opted to look for a bed and breakfast, so that I could shower and wash my grimy clothes. Unfortunately, after rigorous searching on the internet, It became apparent that every bed and breakfast, hotel and hostel in my price range was fully booked in the area. I had a decision to make.

The Isle of Portland section of the coast path is 13 miles long and to include this in the days' walk would mean ending it close to Weymouth. Before starting the hike I'd made the strict decision to never camp near a built up area and so, with an element of regret, I thought it best to advance through Weymouth without delay, reaching a more rural area to the north west of Chesil Beach.

After an arduous hour or two of road walking, it was a relief to finally be hiking alongside the coast once more and I took half an hours break at Chickerell Hive Point, boiling up some water on my stove and relaxing with a refreshing cup of coffee. My thoughts were still firmly affixed on where I would be camping for the night and while pondering my options, I wondered if it was worth trying accommodation further afield. It was another eight miles on the trail and would mean a distance of nearly twenty miles for the day, but I dialled a number for a bed and breakfast in the village of Abbotsbury. To my surprise, they had a single room free and with elation, despite a cost of seventy pounds, I confirmed the reservation. I now had a focus for the rest of the evening, happy in the knowledge that I had a comfy bed waiting for me, and a shower.

It was almost 4pm and I had eight more miles to trek, slightly inland across fields and through gentle woodland and ending in a very scenic ridge walk overlooking rolling hills and beyond to the picturesque St. Catherine's Chapel, which stood proudly above the village. Although I was a little annoyed at myself for having to miss a section of the path, the choice to stay in Abbotsbury was a good one.

I arrived at the Swan Inn around 7.30pm, still very aware of my stench, and was asked to wait in the bar area until one of the staff had inspected the room and brought me the key. I sampled a pint of local ale in a quiet corner, away from the noses of the clientele, but it wasn't too long before the pub filled with new arrivals and the net was closing in around me. A couple approached my table, seeing that three of the chairs were unoccupied and asked if they could sit. In a welcoming tone, but highly self-conscious about whether they'd regret their decision, I offered the seating with a pleasant and simple "Yes, of course". They turned out to be very friendly and we chatted for some time about my hike and the fact that I should have been in America trekking the Pacific Crest Trail, if it hadn't have been for the pandemic. It was the first time I'd conversed with people at length since the previous morning when Noel had left, and my worries about the smell of my damp clothes disappeared.

Eventually, the conversation was interrupted by a staff member bringing my room key. As much as I had enjoyed talking to the couple, it was time to leave them and do some chores, washing clothes in the shower and hanging them to dry overnight in my room. By the time I returned to the bar for an evening meal, they were seated elsewhere and so I took the opportunity to consume a large plate of Lasagne in the pub garden, washed down with another pint of beer. Clothes washed, myself washed and fed, and a night in a comfy warm bed, tomorrow was sure to be a great day.

AUGUST 15TH

Trudging through wet shale on an endless beach is not only frustrating when carrying sixteen kilograms on your back, it's downright annoying, but there was no other option for well over two miles towards West Bexington. To top off my agony, it began to rain heavily and there was no shelter in sight, so I was grateful for my trekking umbrella, which kept my head and shoulders dry, if not my newly-washed trousers. The rain was one thing, but the scrunch of the shale beneath my feet was an audible nightmare. Every footstep sounding like a hard brush sweeping water from a concrete surface, a noise which has always sent an almighty shiver up my spine and makes the hairs on my arms stand on end. To make matters worse, I wasn't the only person on the beach. There seemed to be constant waves of crunching gravel sounds from all directions, like an army of maracas were shooing me away. I would normally have been relieved to eventually escape the infernal noise, when crossing a small wooden bridge and heading across an open grassy field, were it not for the increase in water pelting me from the skies. Past the holiday village near Burton Bradstock, i endured a relentless pounding of hard rain and hail, and a total sludge-fest underfoot. Amazingly, It didn't seem to put off the bustling crowds at West Bay, as I appeared to them over the top of East Cliff, frustrated and very damp to say the least.

West Bay is small and tightly packed around a quaint harbour, but it gave the impression of being much larger, probably due to it being in proximity to the town of Bridport and the ease of access which major roads provide. I have since learned that it was a location for the British television drama 'Broadchurch', and now I understand why it was so busy, even in poor weather.

I was in need of food after the exhaustion of the gravel beaches and chose a small seafront stand to restock. I didn't choose particularly wisely though. I'd already passed a number of stalls and open-fronted shops that heaved with hungry daytrippers. Pasties, chips and cream cakes were on offer in abundance at these places, but I realised very quickly that my chosen eatery only offered a slim selection of fare. Reluctantly purchasing a yoghurt covered flapjack and an orange flavoured iced lolly because I was in no mood to queue elsewhere, I then moved on, crossing the graceful, undulating fields that surrounded Thorncombe Beacon and Seaton and on towards one of the highest points on the South West Coast Path, Golden Cap.

Golden Cap is a steep climb from all sides. A glorious pinnacle that dominates the landscape for miles around and is the highest point on the south coast of England. I was thankful for steps being built on the approach from the east as the weather was still pretty grim, and I ascended on slippery mud in a grey haze of drizzle through the trees, finally poking my head out onto the summit and admiring as much of the view as the elements would allow. It certainly wasn't the day to be taking extended breaks, every possible seating spot was soaked. With views limited in all directions, I took one photograph of the trig point, with my hiking pole propped against it for proof I was there, and I prepared to descend. As I turned, two hikers approached from the west. They were thru hikers and had been on the trail for a staggering number of days, hiking in the opposite direction and nearing the end of their journey. I was so pleased to have met these people, a lady and gentleman a few years older than me and two of the nicest people I had met so far. We talked about hiking stuff, as hikers customarily do, and they imparted their accrued wisdom upon me, telling of diversions in place further along the trail and how to avoid them. A couple of these diversions sounded ominous, stealthfully sliding underneath a locked gate for one thing, and walking along a treacherous section of path that had almost collapsed a couple of hundred feet into the sea below. I wasn't even sure exactly where they meant and when I would happen upon this mission either. Somewhere around the St. Austell area. Time will tell, I thought, as I tried to store all the relevant information in my spinning head. I said my goodbyes, wishing them well for their final few days and continued on my way.

Unsure of an exact location for camping that night, I was thankful that the rain had stopped and there were plenty of open fields before me. Unfortunately, they were either farmers fields or were just too uneven to pitch a tent on. As the sunlight began to fade, I chanced upon one of the only flat areas of land that i'd seen since leaving Golden Cap. It was sheltered behind tall bushes and had a wonderful view of the sea and surrounding hills that i'd just walked across, including of course, Golden Cap. The only problem was, it was right on the coast path. This was the first time i'd camp so close to the main path and was therefore a little apprehensive, but I waited the day out while enjoying a rather tasty dehydrated meal and a mug of coffee, before swiftly pitching my tent in the half-light. Curling up snuggly in my warm, goosedown sleeping bag as the days light finally gave in to the night, I closed my eyes and listened for the sweeping sounds of the waves on the warm late evening breeze, and the haunting harmonies of cattle lowing in distant fields.

AUGUST 16TH

The following day was full of expectation for me. I would be crossing into a new county and was very excited about it. I was still a fair few miles from the border, but the section between my camp spot and Axemouth harbour held a new fascination, a six mile woodland walk that I had been told was quite prehistoric in its nature. This was the Jurassic coast after all and I was sure I wouldn't be disappointed. I still had to pass through Charmouth and Lyme Regis however, and having camped upon the coast path itself the previous night, I'd had to be up at the crack of dawn before I was discovered by any disgruntled farmers or dog walkers, and so my timings were a little thrown off.

It was barely 7am and the tide was still washing ferociously upon the shore between the two coastal villages and wouldn't reveal the beach (which was the shortest and fastest route) until 10am at the earliest. Needing to fill up my water bottles, I thought it best to head into Charmouth itself to find a shop while I waited for the tide to ebb. Amenities were a little sparse to say the least, especially before 8am on a sunday morning, and my inland exploration provided absolutely nothing of value, yet my stubbornness dictated I continue, even though it was a constant uphill road through the village. So, I'd walked extra yards and ascended steadily, all without gain and for absolutely nothing more than killing time. After very little consideration, I think my pride got the better of me and instead of turning around and heading back towards the shore to wait for the waters to recede, I continued on....and up!

What seemed like an eternity of acclivity along traffic-filled main roads, through woodlands and across a golf course fairway, I finally entered Lyme Regis, exhausted and pouring with sweat in the humidity of the morning. A Tesco Express store along the main shopping street was a sight for sore eyes. I purchased more water and snacks for the woodlands ahead of me, and a warm cheese and bacon pastry made a welcome change from porridge and chocolate bars. Checking the weather radar on my phone while consuming two half-sized cans of Coca Cola (for some reason it worked out cheaper that way) I noticed a weather front moving in from the south.

The red tract that swept across my phone screen indicated rain...very heavy rain in fact, and it looked like it was going to be upon me in less than half an hour. With this in mind, it made sense to head to the woodland stretch of the trail as soon as possible and hope the canopy above would give me extra cover. It did, but it created a different world altogether, one of high humidity and a mist that seemed to emanate from behind every thicket, wetting me as thoroughly as if there were no leaves overhead at all. Deeper and deeper into the woodland, I meandered through bosk and underwood, over tree roots and around murky, green pools of stagnant water. I half-expected to see a velociraptor gnawing through a primeval carcass as I passed archaic shrubs and large, pointed ferns. It was eerie, but incredible. Wide-eyed, I navigated the twisting path for six long miles, stopping only once at the half way point to read a sign that told me just that. The rain continued to fall throughout my leafy three hour journey until I finally reached the woodlands' conclusion and into an interesting section known as Goat Island and the Great Chasm.

It was in 1839 on christmas day, that a huge landslip occurred in the area. It is referred to as 'The Great Slip' and is the largest ever to have happened in this area.

The dampness and constant abrasion of wet socks on soft skin was beginning to take its toll and I was so thankful to see blue skies and sunshine at the other end of the wood, and more importantly a bench, where I seated my soggy rear and let my bare feet feel the warm breeze. I dressed my poorly, red toes with plasters and talcum powder and enjoyed the afternoon sun and the intriguing view of the landslip with a snack, before setting off once more through copse and cornfields and across the border into south Devon.

SOUTH DEVON

AUGUST 16TH, CONTINUED...

I didn't notice any signage informing me of my crossing into Devon. It was only after arriving in the village of Seaton that something in the back of my mind alerted me to a change of postal code. Double-checking on a temperamental internet connection, my phone confirmed I had indeed crossed the border and my first county was completed. It was quite a thrill actually.

With a beaming smile upon my face, which a passing family of four must have thought quite creepy as they shuffled their youngsters past me at speed, I studied the coastal section around Seaton Bay from my vantage point, and I gazed upon the village of Beer, standing proudly atop the cliff and overlooking the bustling Seaton Beach. It was mid-afternoon and the mornings rain was now just an afterthought for tourists and locals alike. What was clearly a mission for many, to enjoy this weather window while it lasted and walk upon a damp beach with an ice cream, mine had a different focus, to have a pint of beer....in Beer! 'Oh, what a tale to tell' I mused, not even considering that a thousand people may well have adopted the same train of thought before me. That wasn't going to stop me though, and off i trudged, opting for an inland path rather than fight my way through the hordes along the beach front.

Unfortunately, my chosen path took me on a rather long road walk up a steep hill, before turning left towards the sea again and to the pub. It was an arduous half an hour but at least it was dry, and I dreamed of a sea view from a pub bench with a cool, refreshing pint of lager, a reward for the days' efforts in poor weather.

Upon arriving at the pub with great anticipation, it was soon clear that my tastebuds would have to wait. There was a queue of people stretching right down the street. Obviously, the pandemic had made attending public places a little more difficult and with the introduction of 'social distancing' and a two metre rule in place, there was a limited amount of space inside the pub. I would have been waiting there for the best part of an hour, and so reluctantly, I pushed on towards Beer Head, where the coast took a ninety degree turn right and on to Branscombe.

I chose the upper path that crossed South Down Common, partly due to the number of people I could see walking along Hooken Cliffs below. That was the proper coast path, but the cliff top was a very pleasant section of coastline, and I took a fifteen minute break to rest my tiring calves and to have a bite to eat, with a stunning view of Sherborne Rocks and a number of trawlers gliding casually along the horizon.

Feeling rejuvenated after a few chocolate snacks, it was a fairly conventional stroll for the next few miles. A steep drop down to Branscombe Mouth and past a bar that, to my disappointment, was temporarily closed, and then to a tough, leg-burning climb that took me into a gentle woodland section.

Echoing chimes of church bells from Branscombe village in the valley below reminded me that there were still places along the coast that were free of tourism and the tranquility enveloped me with a comfort I'd not felt for quite a while. I wasn't focusing on where I'd been or where I was heading, I was in the moment, absorbing myself with the sounds and smells that surrounded me. Summer flowers in a multitude of colours, dotted sporadically within a sea of swaying woodland grass, and trees that seemed to lower their creaking bows to welcome me on an amiable breeze. The late afternoon ambience was almost tangible.

As I emerged from the cover of trees near Berry Cliff, the trail once again hugged the cliff tops. To the left of me, a glittering expanse of sea stretching as far as the eye could see, and to my right beyond a barbed wire fence, flat harvested cornfields and farmland. The narrow, earthy trail eventually gave way to undulating grassy fields and a very strange sight indeed:

There were three vehicles parked haphazardly in the middle of a large field. They were not typical vehicles for the terrain either and I instantly dismissed farmers,

49

landowners or even hunters. I was unsure as to the whereabouts of the owners and this made me a little nervous, as they looked like city-types, and city folk on the coast at dusk could surely mean only one thing in my mind, a beach party! With alert levels on high, I shuffled stealthfully past the cars, a pristine black BMW and two smaller sporty numbers, and with sufficient distance between, I turned to observe the situation once again.

A spiralling wisp of smoke from the gorse bush on the edge of the field caught my attention. From a new angle I could clearly make out a chimney on a tin roof. It was a cabin set high on the cliff tops and without a doubt the location of the vehicle owners. I was somewhat annoyed by the permanent dwelling though, as the fields around this area were perfect for wild camping, but with the possibility of being spotted by a group of drunken or potentially mischievous youths as they left their coastal hideaway in their snazzy cars did not fill me with comfort, though I almost took the risk at one point, until a loud snort from a pig farm on the adjacent field seemed to warn me otherwise.

The evening light was beginning to fade and I reached a point-of-no-return on the trail. There was a steep drop which disappeared into thick woods at the base of a valley. If I were to continue and there was nowhere to camp, I would either have to push on into the unknown and the darkness, or turn around and climb back up the hill (also in darkness) using energy that would be best conserved for the following day. My best option was the field to my right. It was very flat and recently harvested, but camping anywhere in the field would mean being in clear view of anyone walking the coast path, and also the farmer that owned it. As I pondered my choices, a mist descended over the area in the dampening evening. It shrouded me in a matter of minutes and made any camping spot within the field completely hidden, for now at least. It was almost like the decision had been made for me and was very strange how it happened so suddenly, and right on cue. Shrugging my laden shoulders I climbed over the fence, crossed the rutted field and began to pitch my tent under a large oak tree. The evening was peaceful, except for the rustling of some burrowing creatures in the hedgerow beside me. What they were I will never know, but it didn't affect my nights sleep.

AUGUST 17TH

It was another early rise due to my location the following morning. The sun was beating down across the cropped hay and was so bright I could barely see. I had to force myself up and out of the tent, as I had done on many occasions before, but this time I was thankful I did. Not one minute had passed since the last item was packed away in my rucksack, before I heard the rumble of a farmers tractor, and through the gate in the far corner of the field he appeared, bouncing on his seat, trying desperately to grip the steering wheel as he was thrown from side to side in his tiny cockpit over the rough, ploughed field. I craftily slipped away along the hedge, hoping that the morning rays would shield me from the farmers view. I climbed the fence and was once again on the coast path, safe from any hostility.

With a decent internet signal on my phone the previous evening, I had been checking the weather forecasts for the coming days. It wasn't looking too promising, with heavy rain and winds set to hit the area within the next 24 hours. I had had the foresight to book myself into a small hotel in Sidmouth for a couple of nights to wait out the worst of it. Not only that, but to give a few muscle tweaks and small blisters time to heal, and to do some laundry, as I stunk quite badly once again. The check-in time wasn't until about 3pm in the afternoon and an early rise meant I had plenty of time to kill, and not too many miles to cover. I had food and water fully stocked and with the morning looking like it was going to be very pleasant and warm, I chose to walk down the steep path to the beach at Weston Mouth.

Being up so early, I arrived on the sunny sands before even the hardiest of dog walkers had appeared. I found a nice seating area where people quite obviously, judging by the litter, had had parties in recent nights. Burned out throw-away barbeques and beer cans were strewn in the dunes. I was apprehensive about sitting there to start with, but I couldn't resist the view out to sea and threw my pack to the ground near a heap of mangled plastic and discarded newspapers. As the first people drifted onto the sands a little while later, it became clear to me that I may have looked like a homeless tramp to them. A loner, sitting amongst the clutter of waste on a seemingly otherwise pretty beach. As the stares continued into the morning, my cares lessened. I had my headphones on, listening to relaxing music, and I enjoyed a warming sunrise and wonderful view across the shining sea. For four hours I sat in the same position, only moving to retrieve my stove for the odd coffee and snacks from my pack. I was completely at ease and the only thing that forced me to set off back to the trail was the threat of rain moving in within the next three hours.

Plans for a lethargic stroll to the hotel had to be re-evaluated the moment I stepped off the beach. A sign, which I hadn't noticed earlier in the morning, stated that the section of trail between Weston Mouth and Sidmouth was closed due to a landslip. Not knowing exactly where the closure was, I didn't want to take any chances and plotted a course through woodlands towards the inland village of Weston. It was a two mile diversion with quite a bit of road walking along narrow, high-hedged lanes, past pretty houses in the quaint village of Salcombe Regis and through the Sidmouth donkey sanctuary, before I was finally back to the cliff tops just a mile along the coast, where I was able to see the extent of the landslip on Higher Dunscombe Cliff. I have since found out that the closure only related to the beach section of coast and the coast path itself was not affected. It wasn't such a big deal I supposed. I still had an hour or so to kill before I could check in at the hotel and the extra miles of walking was no problem considering I was about to take a full rest day on my butt. The only issue was the weather. The diversion had taken me nearly an hour of inland navigation and the clouds had begun to gather ominously above me. It wasn't much longer before the first signs of lousy weather were upon me and my first few steps into Sidmouth itself were soggy to say the least. By the time I had reached the hotel, I was saturated from head to toe.

I arrived at the hotel reception desk prematurely, possibly an hour early, but I hoped that my sodden appearance would instil a little empathy from the owners and they would allow me into my room before the check-in time. Thankfully, they were very welcoming and somewhat sympathetic to my situation.

After relieving myself of the weight upon my back, I was taken on a brief tour of the hotel and its facilities: A luxurious dining area with elegantly laid tables, catering for groups of all sizes. A small, but fully stocked self-service bar and lavish leather sofas in a grand conservatory, with French doors that opened out to an extensive covered patio area and well tendered garden. It was wonderful, and I hadn't even stepped foot into my room yet. There were a few protocols to follow in light of the current pandemic, but it wasn't too long before I was in my very cosy single room, unpacking my wet gear and taking a hot shower to expel the chill inside of me. I also took my dirty clothes into the cubicle with me, rinsing them thoroughly in the near-scalding soapy water before wringing them out as best I could and hanging them to dry in every space I could find in the room. I was happy to smell freshness again. The grime from the previous few days had begun to infest every inch of my being.

I'd seen many videos of thru-hikers on youtube prior to starting my own hike and always found it fascinating when I saw them wash clothes in a bath tub, seeing the clear warm water turn chocolate brown in a matter of seconds. I never really thought it could be as bad as it looked....but it is! It's almost impossible to get every last molecule of muck out of clothes in a shower, and unfortunately, no matter how long I washed or how often I rinsed, the stench was always going to hang around. With a day of doing absolutely nothing ahead of me, I realised this could be my opportunity to figure out a way of doing laundry on trail and be the most unblemished, fresh-smelling thru-hiker that had ever graced the South West Coast Path. Now my day off had a purpose and there was even an element of excitement about it. I realised each day before this had truly become just a routine of walking, eating and sleeping, but this was set to change as I now had a mission, one day to create, to invent, some kind of clothes washing system that would keep me smelling lemon-fresh and spare me the embarrassment every time I interacted with the general public.

After a truly delicious three course meal and a couple of cold beers in the hotel restaurant, I retired to my bedroom for the evening, where I switched on the television to watch the local news and ponder my laundry situation. I decided to buy some gel packets, which are normally thrown into a washing machine in lieu of powder or detergent. Searching online, I chose a brand that could be purchased from the local Tesco Express, which was a gentle five minute walk down the road from the hotel. I already had a large clear ziploc bag, which would hold at least two shirts, a couple of pairs of socks and my trekking pants, and with a litre of water would be sufficient to create a semblance of a portable washing machine.

The relaxing nature of my morning on the beach, the wonderful meal, the hot shower and the two beers took their toll, and I drifted into slumber within a short space of time. Any further ideas regarding my washing plan would have to wait til the following day.

AUGUST 18TH

The morning came as quickly as the evening had passed. I opened my eyes to a beam of soft warming sunlight through a gap in the curtains and heard the low rumble of rush hour traffic on the street beyond my ground floor bedroom window. Glancing at the clock, I had woken several minutes before my alarm had sounded. I felt refreshed and ready to enjoy my day of rest, which began with breakfast in the hotel restaurant. A full English was on the cards. Bacon, sausage, eggs, beans, fried bread and mushrooms were all washed down with freshly squeezed orange juice and a cup of tea, and after a warm shower I was all set for the day ahead.

A heavy rain shower had temporarily cleared the local area of holiday-makers and I sauntered into town through semi-deserted streets. With an empty backpack, I headed straight for the household section of the local store. During my search for the gel packets along the fully stocked shelves, I noticed something that had not crossed my mind the previous evening. Scented laundry additives. They are designed to add extra fragrance to a wash, but the smell was quite potent even before placing them into water. For the sake of a few extra pounds on my shopping bill, I deemed it beneficial to my smelly laundry conundrum and tossed them into my basket. My thinking was, that a few items of clothing in a plastic bag, along with a few of these scented balls, would produce an aroma of freshly laundered clothes, even if they were slightly dirty. And so, with a twenty-wash box of gel packets and a new box of ziploc bags to hold these items in my backpack, I was all set, and I hoped this would see me through at least a couple of stinky weeks on trail.

My first test with the new system came as soon as I returned to the hotel. One of my shirts seemed to take a lot longer to dry than other items of clothing, and as such, the stench festered if it was left for too long in a damp place, such as the old teak wardrobe i'd hung it in, for instance! I threw the shirt into a new ziploc bag and poured in some laundry additives, closed it up and scrunched the hell out of it, releasing a redolence of fabricated lavender that not only coated the moist shirt, but everything else within a six feet radius. I did the same to a number of other items that i'd washed the night before, ones that had already dried upon the two small radiators on the bedroom walls.

Feeling pleased with my efforts, I donned a newly laundered shirt in readiness for an afternoon beer in the hotel conservatory. It wasn't until I had sat down on one of the comfortable sofas in the bar area, that I suddenly became very aware of the potent stench of lavender. It was all I could smell and it was embarrassingly strong. Thankfully, the bar was quite empty of people. Just a family playing pool several feet away, but I remember thinking to myself that they must be able to smell me, even from that distance. I decided to finish the rest of my beer outside in the sunshine, in the hope that the gentle breeze would take some of the fragrance away. It did not!

It was late afternoon and I'd enjoyed three cold beers before deciding to check the weather forecast for the following day. Continuous rains that were predicted had not yet arrived and I was a little concerned that I may still end up getting soaked through and my two nights at the hotel would have been in vain. The forecast looked grim. It was at this point I decided to enquire about staying for one more night. It was going to be an expensive few days for me, especially as I was told I'd have to switch to a larger, pricier room due to another booking for the room I was already in. I pondered my options and chose to stay at the hotel, despite the possibilities of finding new accommodation a lot cheaper elsewhere. I felt comfortable and I was enjoying my stay, the hospitality and the great food. To top it all off, the kind hosts offered to wash my clothes too, free of charge, and although I'd spent a while scrubbing and wringing everything in the shower the night before, the chance to have a full pack of freshly laundered clothes was irresistible.

AUGUST 19TH

I had to vacate my groundfloor room by 10am the following morning for cleaning purposes. I was unable to transfer to my new room until that had also been cleaned and so I had a four hour window to fill. Unfortunately for me, the heavy rain that had been anticipated by the Met Office was now making an appearance from the south west. I suppose I could have spent the time sat in the bar, or gone in search of a cafe in the town, but I chose to get my legs moving again and headed for the wooded area of Bulverton Hill, just to the north west of Sidmouth. I've always enjoyed walking through a wood in pouring rain and with nothing to carry but my brolly and a bottle of water, it made the experience even more enjoyable. I'd made a good choice. My legs were feeling great, the blisters on my toes had healed nicely and my sense of well-being was bountiful. Even being lashed by the spray from an angry tide as I passed Jacob's Ladder on the Sidmouth seafront, could not dampen my spirits. I may have been drenched once more, but knowing that

I had one extra night in a cosy, warm bed made all the difference.

Another incredible evening meal and the most amazing mushroom soup I have ever tasted made for a fitting end to my stay at the Woodlands Hotel. The expense had dented my budget for the trip, but I had no regrets at all. This journey was supposed to be an adventure of a lifetime and my three nights of luxury only enhanced the experience. It was with a heavy heart that I finally had to say goodbye and continue my hike.

AUGUST 20TH

It was a bright, warm morning as I set off along the coast once again towards Budleigh Salterton. It was a cheerful seven miles along sweeping cliff tops and through amiable woodlands until reaching the Otter Estuary nature reserve, where the trail cut sharply inland for a brief period before emerging on the Budleigh seafront. The mid-morning sun was high in the sky and a cooling sea breeze fanned the myriad of tourists sauntering along the promenade.

Amidst the hordes of clean, well dressed tourists, I fixed my eye upon someone that didn't quite fit the sightseer stereotype. He sat upon a bench, with his right ankle placed in a manly ninety degree pose on his other knee, and his right arm was flung casually across the top of the seat. He was dressed in a light blue checked shirt with sleeves rolled up to his elbows and a dusty brown cap. Beside him, placed with precise attention and care, a backpack.....clearly a fellow hiker, and I knew instantly that he was walking the coast path too.

There seems to be an intuition between backpackers, like a beacon or radar that alerts you immediately of their presence amongst any amount of people. I could have spoken to many people that morning with just a simple 'hello' and gotten no reply at all, but there's an empathy between hikers that extends beyond simple appreciation of each others' journeys. There's a connection, a like-mindedness that separates us from the tourists milling around us. I felt compelled to venture over to where he sat and introduce myself.

As I approached the bench the guy smiled. He was obviously aware that our paths were alike, albeit mine was in the opposite direction to his. We exchanged a few trail stories and imparted knowledge of gear and wild camping locations. He told me he was recording clips of people that he'd met along the way and asked if I would be happy to appear in the video he would be creating on his return home. How could I refuse? Awkwardly, as I always am in front of a camera, I attempted a smile and a brief wave of the hand towards the lens, but then I froze, suddenly aware of the crowds walking past me, probably wondering what was going on. Did he want me to speak? I wasn't sure, yet he seemed to be filming me for a lot longer than I was expecting. Maybe he was anticipating a few words explaining what I was doing and why I was doing it, though after what seemed like an eternity, he slapped his viewfinder back into place on the camera body and simply said "thanks". I recently found the short documentary he made for his Youtube channel and was flattered to see myself included amongst the happy throng of hikers he had met before me. None of them had said anything on their clips either, which I was relieved about.

The coast path out of Budleigh was another ascent, as so often was the case after every village. I passed yet another golf course and had to walk through another holiday park, something all too familiar to me now, although this time I was taken aback by gunfire echoing around the caravans and static homes. A little unnerved, I stopped in my tracks to ascertain what was going on. After checking the map, I was relieved to notice I was close to Straight Point rifle range. I thought it strange to have a firing range so close to a holiday park. It was hardly a relaxing location to spend a family vacation and it certainly wasn't very relaxing for me for a couple of minutes. As I passed the main gate, a guard in army fatigues gave me a hard stare, to which I felt like smiling sarcastically but thought better of it.

Passing Sandy Bay and the High Lands of Orcombe, which sounded to me like a kingdom found in a J.R.R Tolkien novel, I reached the Geoneedle at Orcombe

Point. Its an impressive stone pyramid nearly five metres high and marks the beginning of the Jurrasic Coastline, which stretches all the way back to Old Harry Rocks in Dorset, from whence I departed just over a week before. I had now completed more than one hundred miles of trail and this was the first big accomplishment of the journey. The next one was soon to arrive as I neared the town of Exmouth, the first ferry crossing of many to negotiate.

The trail into Exmouth was more than a mile of road walking, past ice cream stands, beachside bars and souvenir stalls. The place was heaving with tourists and I was relieved to reach the ferry terminal. I'd arrived about forty five minutes too early and there was no queue of people waiting to board, so I chose to duck into a bar that sat on the harbour itself. As I sipped my cold beer, I watched nervously as a line of people slowly began to form adjacent to the harbour wall. I'd read on the Starcross Ferry website that due to coronavirus restrictions, there were a limited number of spaces per trip. I wasn't taking any chances and couldn't afford to sit and wait for another hour, so I guzzled my beer as quickly as I could, until I felt a slight bloating in my stomach. Embarrassingly, the gases had built up and were in desperate need of release in the form of a large belch, which I did well to keep as quiet as possible in the midst of several drinkers that surrounded me. Suddenly finding it slightly uneasy to move with a pint of alcohol swishing around my innards, I gingerly rolled myself off the chair, hefted my pack onto my shoulders and joined the ever-growing number of people in the queue. I was about fifteenth in line and although I had to stand awkwardly for quite some time before the ferry arrived, I was happy knowing that I'd be catching the next trip across the estuary.

I alighted the ferry in Starcross about 4pm and began the long road walk that ran parallel with the train line. It was not a particularly pleasant experience if I'm brutally honest, and knowing that finding any kind of camp spot along this section of coast was going to be very difficult indeed, only made matters worse. After four miles of gruelling concrete, past scruffy brick buildings and cheesy holiday parks, I arrived in the centre of Dawlish. There was a sense of unease as I sat on a bench near the main bus stop while pondering my best move for the evening. I remember the hiker in Budleigh telling me of one particular camp spot near Watcombe, just north of Torquay, but that would mean another nine miles of walking with no guarantee that I would find the area that he mentioned, and time was against me. Even though I'd just spent three nights in a luxurious hotel, the decision to search for another bed and breakfast seemed to be my best option, and so speedily, I did.

After working for a lengthy ten years as a delivery driver, making stops all over the United Kingdom, I considered myself quite the human road atlas. Unfortunately, in my haste to find suitable accommodation for the evening in the local area, I made a very big error. For some reason I had it in my head that the next town on the coast from my current position was Paignton and I was quite proud of myself for finding a bed and breakfast in that area for a very reasonable price. After consulting the map to find the exact location, I was distraught to notice that I had booked a room some fifteen miles and two bus journeys away. The booking was non-refundable and I knew I'd be missing a huge section of trail, but there was still a part of me that found some relief in the fact that I had a bed for the night. It was getting to it that was causing a problem.

Time was pushing on and the days light was beginning to fade as my first changeover dropped me in the centre of Torquay at nearly 8.30pm, with at least another fifteen minutes of waiting time before the number 12A bus would appear and whisk me away from the undercurrent of violence that surged from every pub doorway in the vicinity.

I rang the bed and breakfast doorbell at 9.30pm. It had been two hours since I made the booking and the owners had attempted to phone me several times, wondering where I was. It turns out I had provided the wrong number in my eagerness to confirm the room, but with no harm done, I climbed into a creaking bed in a compact box room and closed my eyes. Even the heavy rain and gusty winds that swept through the region later that night could not wake me from my slumber.

AUGUST 21ST

With a fully stocked backpack of food, I opted to press on early the following morning and declined what was probably a wonderful breakfast. In and out of the room within ten hours, I grinned at the fact I'd paid five pounds per hour for my stay at the bed and breakfast. The easiest money the owners had probably ever made, but the most welcomed nights sleep I had had for some time and I didn't regret it for one second. I'm not sure I even regretted missing fifteen miles of trail in a built-up area. I'm not a purist when it comes to hiking and I didn't feel the need to have stepped on every inch of trail, it's the experience that counts, in my book, and I was certainly getting plenty of that.

Despite a brisk wind from the southwest, I rather enjoyed everything the trail had to offer that day. I was fresh, showered and still had a pack full of clean clothes having not camped since Sidmouth.

Brixham is a busy fishing village that hit the nostrils before I even hit the streets. Lengthy queues of fish lovers awaited their turn at the fish market and as I passed, the smell of the sea enveloped me. It was over-powering in the warmth of the morning sun and caused a brief shiver as the saline molecules attacked me from all angles. The trail took me around the compact harbour, which was overlooked by colourful houses on the surrounding hills. The vibrancy was quite over-whelming and there was so much to take in, I almost had a sensory overload. A cafe with a long seating area was filled with morning coffee drinkers and a lovely aroma of freshly-baked croissants competed with the whiff of salty sea, which lapped gently against the myriad of bobbing sailing boats, anchored in the harbour water.

For the first time in quite a while, the trail was quite tame as I left the town and headed towards Berry Head and its lighthouse, that stood high on the peninsula. I was aware that the weather forecasters had predicted strong winds for the south west in the coming days, but as yet, they hadn't materialised and the hike was very pleasant in warm sunshine. The scenery was stunning as I headed further south, past Scabbacombe Sands and Outer Froward Point, and I stopped a number of times to admire the views and take energy-reviving breaks.

While I sat on one particular grassy knoll, that provided a breath-taking view of the Mew Stone, a small and rocky outcrop just off the coast, my attention was drawn to a couple of figures, moving wearily through the gorse on the opposite bank. I watched intently for a minute or two and I could just make out that they both carried large rucksacks. Clearly hikers and both travelling in the same direction as me. As much fun as it had been to travel with another hiker on the first day of the journey, I was now relishing my solo adventure and didn't want to be lumbered with new people at this stage, and so I waited for another half hour to give them time to put some distance between us. Unfortunately, this was pointless, as they had also decided to stop just over the hill, and I caught them up within a very short time. As I approached them, I prepared myself for the inevitable hiker conversation, but I was quite thankful to simply receive a brief greeting as I passed. In fact, one of the guys didn't even acknowledge my existence. It was clear from that moment that I wouldn't be spending any amount of time with them and pushed on happily.

As I approached the village of Kingswear through leafy copse and pine woodlands, I passed remains of a World War ll landing craft maintenance site. This area was primarily used for the construction and repair of sea-going vessels needed for Winston Churchill's 'Great Plan' and the D-Day landings in Normandy in 1944. It was quite an eerie feeling to have full access to the crumbling buildings and concrete slipways that would have been so frequently used during the war. To know that so many brave souls had stood in that exact spot and helped our country to victory all those years ago was very humbling. I felt insignificant in these surroundings and I had to hold a tear back as I praised the efforts of all involved with my own minute of silence, in gratitude for what they had done for us.

I was now only a short distance away from the harbour at Kingswear and the ferry crossing that would take me over the River Dart and into the pretty town of Dartmouth. I had spent so long looking around the war site, that on exiting it, the two hikers i'd seen earlier were passing me. Once again, one guy say 'Hi' and the other ignored me. I had a feeling that I'd be sharing the ferry with them both, and that we'd be leapfrogging each other until dusk, and I'd be forced to hike further than I'd hoped so as not to be camping anywhere near them. But my luck was to change as I passed them yet again just yards before the harbour. One of the guys had a problem with his pack and they had stopped to re-arrange it. Swiftly, I pressed on, saying hello for a third time to the sociable guy, while his friend lowered his head and pretended I wasn't there, and I reached the ferry just in time. I was literally seconds away from missing the connection and as I sat down, the ferryman unhooked the heavy rope and we set sail for the opposite bank. As we crossed the river, I looked back at the Kingswear bank, and I saw the other hikers approaching the dock. I wouldn't see them again, knowing that it would be at least an hour before they were able to catch the next ferry.

I took a slight detour inland when I alighted in Dartmouth. The map didn't give me hope of finding somewhere to camp near the coast path, and so I took a new direction up an incredibly steep road, heading for the hamlet of Little Dartmouth. It was a fantastic decision. In the failing light, i found a wonderfully sheltered and stealthy corner of a corn field, with a view east across the ocean. I knew the weather was going to be fine in the morning and so I pitched my tent with the thoughts of a beautiful sunrise to look forward to.

AUGUST 22ND

It was saturday morning and the sun was showering me in golden brilliance. It was so bright I could barely see as I peered around the canvas fly sheet. Everything was still and I was well and truly isolated in this section of the corn field. With that in mind, i decided to get the stove out and have a coffee. There was no rush at all as I had another ferry crossing to come at Salcombe. I wouldn't reach that point by the time the ferry ceased in the late afternoon, and so I calculated I had around twenty miles to walk in just over thirteen hours, which would put me somewhere close to the ferry for the morning crossing. I'm no Einstein, but even I was aware that that sounded like a leisurely day at a relatively steady speed. No equation necessary!

I packed my gear away very slowly and very precisely that morning. Everything was in it's right place, stuff sacks were free of air and rolled to perfection. Cooking implements were washed. Even the dirt from my shoes and the bottom of my trekking pants was scraped off, cleansed with a wet wipe and dried in direct sunlight. I even had the time to ponder on my journey so far, while gazing across the gently swaying corn in the field and beyond to the shimmering sea, recording a short vlog for family and friends back home. For the first time I was feeling the sense of freedom that I'd desperately yearned for and I needed to tell someone.

Days were beginning to merge together, so much so, it was hard to work out whether it was a week day or not without consulting my calendar. My internal clock was now guided by the setting and rising of the sun and my thoughts were constantly fixed upon mileages, footcare, where to find water and where I would lay my head for the night. I was fast becoming part of nature, part of the landscape. Just a week before I was concerned about what people might think as I brushed past them in my smelly clothes. Now I hardly even noticed these people, yet care what they thought. My focus was on the natural landscape, the rain-bearing clouds, the whisper of winds through the trees and the fresh, salty air. I felt alive, and it was the first morning that I had no doubt in my mind of my intention to complete the trail. After several days of poor weather, the enthusiasm for such a task can be difficult to muster, but with a new sense of vigor brewing inside me, I was confident, excited and thoroughly boosted by everything around me. I was finally content in myself and my choices, to the point that the dazzling sun seemed to warm up my soul and provide me with protection from anything that would be thrown at me along my journey.

It was difficult to leave the solitude that morning, but eventually the decision was made to take the first steps of the day, and I embraced it with zest.

I'd like to thank Avril Lavigne for her contribution to my journey for the following couple of hours or so. Through Little Dartmouth, Stoke Fleming and into the quaint village of Strete, I strutted in time with the Canadian punkster's tunes at full volume. Four album's-worth of songs I played, to which I mimed with immense enthusiasm and tapped my trekking pole upon the narrow, tarmac lanes like an extra long drum stick, devoid of caring what others might think should they happen to peer from their cottage windows as I bounded past. Until that point of the trip, I had carefully chosen music that stimulated my hiking emotions, music that evoked a sense of freedom or was conducive to relaxation through sounds of nature. Boring, you might say! So, you can imagine the change of pace that Lavigne had provided that morning. It was an extra boost to my morale. She may not be everyone's cup of tea, but she's my guilty pleasure!

There was a Post Office in Strete. It was a very tiny store with cramped aisles, loaded with every provision a small village might need. It also stocked plenty of snack foods, ideal for the weary hiker and so, I thought i'd take full advantage. A sign on the door notified customers of restrictions to the number of people allowed in at any time. There were two already inside and that meant I had to wait for a few minutes before entering. I stood next to an elderly lady, who stared with amazement, presumably, at the size and weight of my pack secured between my calves as I rifled through the top pocket in search of my wallet. "Are you hiking?" she enquired, still grimacing in the direction of my lower legs.

"I'm walking the coast path," I replied informatively, expecting an extended conversation with details about my journey so far and my intentions for the days ahead. I was silenced with an abrupt retort:

"You call that fun?" she uttered. I could only snort and force a half-grin of acceptance, knowing that she would never understand my reasons for undertaking such a hike.

Loaded up with a couple of Ginsters peppered steaks, a bar of nougat and a can of Coke, I came across a bench overlooking Start Bay and stopped for a break in the sunshine. I positioned my pack in the hope that the warmth of the sun would dry the damp socks and t-shirt that I'd washed earlier in the morning and which were pegged to my backpack washing line, and I gorged on unhealthy pastries and carbonated drinks to give me some extra energy for the miles in front of me.

I was very close to ending my hike prematurely during that short break and possibly injuring myself severely, or worse, as I stumbled on a rut beside a cliff edge and nearly fell backwards down a sheer drop of nearly 200 feet into trees, thicket and who knows what else. Thankfully, I was able to gather myself swiftly and prevent any further rearward motion. After an extra five minutes gathering my thoughts and lowering my heart rate, I was ready to move on, cautiously.

Slapton Sands is a two mile stretch of unsheltered, flat walking and I remembered the annoyance of the shingle beach near West Bexington and feared the worst. Although it was still relatively annoying, what looked like more of the same from the map legend turned out to be less of a hindrance. Sandy in places, but firm under foot, I stomped confidently and hastily along the 18 inch-wide path, with a stunning view of the Slapton Ley Nature Reserve to the right of me. I was relieved to have walked as quick as I did through that section, not only to be rid of the constant traffic noise along the main road, but to make it to a bird hide at Torcross Point just seconds before a torrential rain storm hit the area.

The rain hit horizontally and lashed the reserves tall reeds into submission, nearly breaking them in two. Pounding the lake, each water droplet that fell from the sky struck so hard, that it seemed to rebound at least two feet off the surface into a colourless haze. I sat for ten minutes in the creaky wooden shack, astounded that the one single cloud above me was able to produce so much water, and then as quickly as it had arrived, it was gone, and the sun once again glinted upon the lake and the moist foliage that hugged its edge.

As I exited my shelter through a dripping doorway, I looked towards the sea. I have no idea where so many people had suddenly appeared from, so soon after the downpour...and they were all dry! I remember comparing them to midges in the Scottish mountains: You think there's none around, then they spring from the grasslands whenever the wind dies (and eat you alive!). Confident I wasn't going to be eaten alive by the beach dwellers, I approached the rocky edges of the sea wall. The luscious aroma of fish and chips had lured me, like the Sirens call, in the direction of a beachside cafe. It had been less than half an hour since I had eaten a substantial meat pie, but I couldn't resist purchasing a childs portion of Britains most loved meal, and promptly scoffed the lot.

For more than three miles the coast ran due south towards the lighthouse at Start Point. It was a rather popular attraction, which I could tell before I'd even arrived due to the location of a car park less than a quarter of a mile away from it. The cliff edge was teeming with sightseers and photographers, it was very picturesque and not difficult to realise why so many people visited. In a prime spot between the cliff and the car park, a young lady sat at the back of her car, boot raised, selling cold drinks. Being uncertain of where my next water source was, I thought it best to stock up, although I should have known what was to come at the first sight of her card machine, and the moment I enquired about the price of her 250ml bottles of dubiously named volcanic spring water, I knew instantly that I'd be digging deep. You can probably buy a two litre bottle of water from a supermarket for around fifty pence, so you can imagine my shock when I was told that a bottle an eighth of the size was going to cost me two pounds each. With the weather being so nice and my supplies running low, I reluctantly bought not one, but three bottles. Six pounds for three quarters of a litre of, what was probably, re-bottled tap water. She obviously thought I was born yesterday, and I gave her no reason to doubt it, but at least the water was chilled and refreshing.

I felt the ferocity of gale force winds as I turned the corner at Start Point Lighthouse. From nothing more than a steady, strong breeze throughout the day so far, being at the most southerly tip of Devon was a shock to the system. Unsheltered from the elements along rocky crags and paths no wider than twelve inches in places, the trail was daunting. I was thankful that the wind was blowing into my face and not forcing me seaward, but it was still a struggle to keep my balance above crashing waves at the foot of dangerously steep coves. There were brief interludes where I was able to catch my breath and take a few photos, but for the most part, it was a difficult couple of hours walking.

There were a few places I'd pinpointed on the map to camp that night, but before I realised it, I was nearing Salcombe and had run out of options. With the evening drawing in, I spotted a flat field overlooking the Salcombe harbour. It was still a little too early to pitch my tent though and I continued along the trail to have a look for more options in a wooded area. Finding nothing flat or free from canvas-tearing bramble, I thought it best to return to the field, which was sheltered by a high hedge and where I would be out of sight from any buildings or people hiking the path. The only way into the field was a climb over a chained metal gate, which happened to be in direct line of sight from a bench, that was positioned perfectly to watch boats entering the harbour below. I was frustrated for over half an hour in dwindling daylight, as a guy and three young boys sat upon the bench admiring the view across the bay. I was tired and hungry and just wanted to pitch my tent, but there was no way I could get over the gate without being seen. Peering over a gorse bush like a meerkat, I checked the situation at regular intervals, especially when it had gone silent, in the hope that the people had gone home, but to my annoyance, it wasn't until the very last light of the evening before they vacated the vicinity and I could swiftly enter the field and pitch up. Thankfully, it was worth the wait. It was a lovely soft pitch, sheltered from any winds and I slept undisturbed.

AUGUST 23RD

Salcombe is a popular and very picturesque resort built on the steep side of the Kingsbridge Estuary. When I say steep, I mean it. I needed to resupply with food and water in the morning and the trek to get to the store was arduous to say the least. After adding a couple of extra kilos of supplies to my pack, things only got worse. How do people come to the decision, opting to live at a forty five degree angle? I imagined the difficulties they must have, not only tending to their gardens, but simply sitting in them. The vision of an elderly lady, abseiling to the greenhouse to re-pot her tomatoes made me chuckle. I spent a long period of time that morning, creating amusing scenarios that local residents might find themselves in within their own four walls. When you're alone for extended periods of time, you have to keep oneself entertained.

Apart from mountaineering in Salcombe for an hour or two, the morning was routine, nothing spectacular to report, except for the stunning views around Sharp Tor and Bolt Head...truly incredible, and with perfect weather to match, I think I was probably in a world of my own for quite some time. That was all to change as I descended past Bolt Tail and entered the congested little coastal village of Outer Hope. A very unpleasant few minutes ensued as I dodged one person after the next in crowded streets. With two car parks in close proximity to the beach, there was an endless queue of traffic attempting to enter the village, without success. This meant they were having to turn around in a very tight space and return in the direction they had come. It wasn't just cars, larger vehicles were trying to manoeuvre too, and with copious amounts of people milling around, it was an absolute nightmare for all involved, and that included me. I'd like to say I was thankful for finding the trail so quickly after the bustle of the roads, but there were so many people heading into the village on the coast path too, that it took almost ten minutes for me to actually step foot on it, having to wait for a sufficient gap in the convoy of tourists due to the path being so narrow. A pleasant enough trail would have lay ahead if it wasn't for stepping to one side to let people pass for the following half hour. These sections of the coast path became very forgettable, very quickly.

Looking at the South West Coast Path Association website, I scrolled down for some details regarding the upcoming ferry crossing over the River Avon estuary at

Bantham. I was alarmed to read that the ferry didn't run on a sunday and cursed the fact I would have an extensive detour, several miles inland to Aveton Gifford. Thankfully, after making new enquiries with a cordial gentleman in charge of the parking facilities, I was informed the ferry was indeed running, and that he would gladly phone ahead to let the ferryman know I was on my way. Well, I was thrilled and grateful all at once, and very relieved to not have any extra mileage added to the day.

I arrived some minutes later to a desolate sand bank. The tide was low and I considered the fact I could have been in the wrong place, been there at the wrong time, or the car park manager had not been truthful to his word, and my heart sank slightly. Then, I heard a cry behind me, and noticed a guy in a wooden boat with an outboard motor. He was clearly waiting for me, it was just a shock to see any vessel being able to take me across the estuary when there was so little water to drive a boat in. As he approached at high speed, I could tell that the water level was so low that he wouldn't be able to get close enough to where I stood, and as he beached the front end a couple of feet away from me, it suddenly became apparent that I would have to span the gulf with my stretched limbs and hope that I didn't fall in. It was rather awkward to say the least, and I was very aware of a few people watching me from the nearby pub, obviously praying that I would face a watery end for their amusement. If I had been just two inches shorter, I may have failed, but as I sprawled between sand and solid bow, with my pack lurching heavily to one side, I just managed to claw my way into the hull.

Safely on board and steadily cruising across the shallow waters, I spotted two people on a sand bank in the middle of the estuary. I assumed they were wanting to catch the ferry and continue on to the same destination as me, the other side of the bay. It turns out that that *was* the other side and these guys were waiting to be ferried back. I had travelled approximately fifty feet and it had cost me a staggering £4.00 for a two minute trip. I was quite taken aback by what had just happened, until I put things into perspective and remembered how far I would have had to walk, the fact it was a sunday and my gratitude for this guy working on a sunday when there were so few people needing to cross the estuary. Despite nearly face-planting in the salty murk, I now regret not giving the guy a tip.

I'd considered buying a pint and a having a bite to eat in Bigbury, on the other side of the estuary, but on my arrival, the location didn't fit my idyllic vision and I thought better of it. It overlooked Burgh Island, and upon it, an eyesore of hideous proportions, the aptly named Burgh Island Hotel. Why an architect would design a building with so little character, paint it 'brilliant white' and place it on a beautiful, lush green peninsula is completely beyond words. I guess I should blame Archibald Nettlefold for the creation in the 1930's and explain to Bigbury, that if it wasn't for him, the village would have had some extra cash, albeit just a tenner for a chilli and chips and a pint of lager.

Bigbury's loss was Challaborough Holiday Park's gain. As I attempted the climb out of the park, I was drawn to the site shop, on the verge of closing for the evening. A store assistant was carrying a sign back inside, one of those that made a terrible squeaking noise in high winds, as it swung in its metal frame. I ventured through the half-closed door and hoped I wouldn't get asked to leave. I wasn't entirely sure what I'd gone in for, but seeing as I'd missed out on a beer in Bigbury, my attention was drawn to the chilled alcoholic beverages, keenly advertised in one section of the store. Knowing they were going to be closing very shortly, my decision making was made easy when my eyes fixed upon a familiar favourite, Kronenbourg.

After carrying a heavy weight on your shoulders for quite some time you get used to it, and so, carrying four cans of lager didn't seem to make that much of an impact at first. Yes, my pack was incredibly heavy, but I was imagining the relaxed evening ahead, in the gentle sunshine with my beers and a warm meal, and so the pain of lugging extra weight had its benefits. What I didn't think about during my rushed decision-making in the site store, was having to carry the empty cans to the next available bin to recycle them. A problem for the next day, I surmised, and concentrated on finding a great camp spot where I could enjoy the cans' contents.

I pitched in a valley, with a view of the tough climb I'd have to endure in the morning. It was relatively close to the path, but with it being a sunday evening, I deduced that only the hardiest of walkers would be coming past at this time of the evening and I knew I wouldn't have any issues with them. It was peaceful, and the only sight of other people was two other hikers at the top of the hill that I would have to summit the next day. I watched with interest as they pitched their two-person tent right on the pinnacle. It was a good spot, albeit a little windier than mine. I raised a beer can in their direction and wished them a good nights sleep.

AUGUST 24TH

The following day was going to be one of the worst days of the entire journey and would have me temporarily doubting the reasons for undertaking such an adventure. It all began to go drastically wrong upon my approach to the River Erme Estuary, where I realised that I'd not checked the tide times recently, or researched how to get across this particular stretch of coastline. Looking at the map and seeing where the coast path crossed and subsequently searching the internet for means of travel, I was devastated to conclude that there was no ferry on this section and to get to the other side of the estuary, I had to walk across at low tide. To my dismay, I had arrived mid-morning and the tide was at it's highest. I sat upon a damp Wonwell Beach and gazed longingly at Owen's Point, just a couple of hundred yards across the bay. I had a choice to make: Do I hang around for the next six hours, until the tide was low enough to wade across the estuary? (even then, I wasn't sure I'd be very comfortable walking through murky sea water up to my knees) or, do I embark on the nine mile inland diversion? After weighing up my two options, I chose the latter. I figured that a nine mile walk on paved roads

92

would take me around three hours, placing me at Owen's Point a lot sooner than if I sat on the beach awaiting the tide to go out. The thought of wading through sea water sent shivers down my spine anyway, so it didn't take me too long to make a choice.

I set off in good spirits and with a bound in my step, intrigued by what lay ahead. I passed a group of canoeists, who were making final preparations to launch their vessels into the flowing estuary waters. I almost asked them if they were interested in making a tenner by ferrying me across to the other side, but I retracted my thought quickly as I noticed it would be impossible to fit two people into such a craft, and a large backpack too. I simply waved and wished them a good morning.

I'd walked for about twenty minutes before deciding to consult the map once again, to make 100% sure that there were no short cuts which would save me valuable time and walking distance. Following the blue line of the estuary inland with my finger, my eyes fixed upon something I hadn't noticed before, a small footbridge. It was a long shot I supposed, but it would significantly reduce the mileage that I had to cover and would mean there was a chance to reach Westbury Point Radar Station before the end of the day, which I'd pinpointed as a very nice spot to wild camp, after watching an online video about it.

A few feet ahead of me, a car appeared from a dusty side road, but stopped completely and didn't look like continuing the journey. I heard a dog bark and concluded the driver had stopped to converse with it's owner, who I couldn't yet see due to high hedge rows lining the thoroughfare. My judgement was affirmed when I peered around the bushes. A middle-aged lady stood in the middle of the road with her dog leashed and bounding around her ankles. She chatted with a gentleman with grey hair and a lengthy grey beard, who sat with one arm out of the car window and was intently nodding to her every word. It was obvious to me they were both local residents and so I thought it might be a good idea to enquire about the footbridge on the map and the paths that led to it. After a brief discussion, the lady assured me that even though the woodlands that surrounded the estuary were private land, I should have no problems walking through them during this time of the day and week. Confidently, I strutted along the single track road with the hope that I was going to have a significantly shortened journey.

The road meandered through thickening woodlands and descended towards the estuary banks. I came across a gate, that the lady had suggested I go through, to continue on a fire track that led deeper into the greenery and would eventually take me to a bridge that spanned a tributary. What she hadn't told me, is that the track passed very close to a house near this particular point and I was a little unsure about continuing. I'd come so far though, and to turn around would be quite deflating. I decided to ignore the house and walk as fast as I could to the bridge, head down, and hope that I wasn't spotted. It was becoming quite a stealth mission and it was only to get worse as I reached another woodland on the other side of the bridge.

Another fire track through denser forest added suspense with every footstep. I was deep inside private land and to be seen now would mean having to answer questions from the landowners, with even the possibility of prosecution for trespassing. It was something I hadn't even considered before passing through the gate earlier.

A gentle rain began to fall through the tree canopy and the humidity increased ten fold within a short time. It was like being in a tropical jungle and my anxiety levels crept up as I realised there was no turning back. As I pushed on cautiously through pools of mud and gravel, the wet bracken saturated the bottom of my trousers, making them feel very heavy. I began to question my choice of route and every time I checked the map, the gps location revealed that I wasn't even half way to the footbridge I'd pinpointed earlier. The day wasn't going well, and it was about to get much worse.

An hour must have passed since the lady had directed me along this path and as I approached a slight rise on the fire track, I heard the rumble of an engine. I froze completely and crouched upon the path, eyes wide open and heart beating frantically, I scanned the gravel road in front of me. My heart sank as I saw the rear lights of a Land Rover glowing in the misty woodland. The vehicle was stationary and I knew it had no place to turn on this track, but where were the occupants? For a few minutes I observed and listened before hearing a door slam shut and seeing the red glow of lights disappear into the murk. I stayed still, listening intently to give me any clues as to the direction of the vehicle, but apart from the dripping foliage around me, all fell eerily and worryingly silent. Will the car return in this direction? Should I continue on this track or head off-road into the undergrowth? My mind was racing and my heart was thumping even harder. I felt like I'd been thrust into the Arnold Swarzenegger film, Predator, but alas, there would be no chopper to fly me to safety in this scenario.

I chose to dive into the wet shrubbery, climbing a steep bank away from the track. Keeping a close eye on my direction of travel, I attempted to forge a new path through bramble and over decaying logs, before I could go no further due to the sheer amount of tangled thorns. For another ten minutes I crouched and listened to near-silence, until my ears detected a faint engine roar on the opposite side of the estuary. 'This must be the Land Rover', I hoped. I pondered my options; staying here in these dank woods for such a time as to be sure the landowners had departed the area or to press on and get out of here as soon as I could. I couldn't travel very fast through the thicket though, I had to return to the track and hope that I could exit the woods as swiftly as possible, albeit another two miles of nervous walking, at least.

I heard the Land Rover constantly for the next half an hour. Thankfully, it was still in the woods across the bay and so I hiked as fast as I could in the sludge. Then suddenly, two sounds that nearly gave me a heart attack, gunfire and dogs barking. The trees had thinned slightly as I hiked ever further north, and so I was extremely concerned that I'd been spotted and the rifles were being pointed towards me. There was no stopping now though. With my heart beating at maximum, I upped the pace even more, only stopping to check my map position at moments I was concealed by greenery. After nearly an hour since first seeing the vehicle, I was nearing the end of the wooded section. The footbridge I'd been heading for initially was completely forgotten and I'd plotted a new path towards a farm, but still had to scale a tall, stone wall and a barbed wire fence to escape the woodlands. With panic but relief in equal measure, I jumped into a large, grassy field filled to the brim with sheep, clearly startled by my unscheduled arrival. There were no footpaths within half a mile of me and so I took a deep breath and headed straight across the open fields, expecting an angry cry from a disgruntled farmer at any moment. It never came. I finally reached the road that I would have been using on the estuary diversion and noticed I was only a couple of miles from the point I'd turned off it...and it had taken me three hours to get there. I decided from that moment on I was going to stick to public roads and not listen to any locals' advice in the future.

I arrived at Owen's Point nearly five hours after choosing the estuary diversion. The tide was still too high to walk across and so I deemed it a small victory, despite the intensity of the past few hours. The rain began to fall but the relief that I felt inside was over-whelming and it didn't dampen my satisfied mood.

I cannot remember whether I'd read it, seen it on the news or been told of its arrival by a friend, but I was aware of a big storm hitting the UK during monday night, with very strong winds and biblical amounts of rain. I'd been camping in storms many times before and so I was fairly confident that, if pitched correctly, my tent would hold firm and I should be able to see it out without major incident. I therefore decided to pitch up late afternoon atop a small hill that overlooked the sea. I'd climbed sufficiently far enough from the coast path, so that I wouldn't be spotted, as I still had at least three hours of daylight left. The mist rolled over the cliffs and shielded me from view too, and with a storm coming, I was sure that nobody else would be out walking the area. With a stiff, warm breeze blowing from the southwest, I pegged my damp clothes upon a barbed wire fence that bordered a grassy farmers field, in the hope they would be dry before it got dark. I made myself a fantastic meal, had a coffee, made sure my tent pegs were secure in the ground and my guylines were tightened, and I closed up the fly sheet to wait for the first rains to arrive. After an emotionally tiring day as well as physical, I fell asleep before the sun had even sunk below the horizon.

AUGUST 25TH:

STORM FRANCIS

I awoke abruptly at 1.30am to the deafening sound of wind and rain lashing upon the tent. I could instantly sense that something wasn't right. There was a strong breeze blowing directly into my face and I could feel the spray of rain water steadily soaking me through. With each gust of wind, there was a rumble as the tent flapped violently around me and in the darkness, it was quite a scary feeling.

I always kept my headtorch within reaching distance during the night, in case I needed something inside the tent, or needed to pee, and as I felt for it in the inner pocket of the tent, I felt the wet canvas whipping my arm. This was bad. This meant something had given way; a guyline, a pole...was the fly sheet still intact? I began to panic, and my fears were justified as I pressed the switch on my torch, and the strong beam of light from my forehead revealed the extent of the damage.

My tent was erected using two poles, which were crossed in the centre and inserted into each opposite corner of the tent inner. The wind was so strong, that the poles had bent over and nearly collapsed on top of me, due to the force of the wind on the fly sheet. The whole tent was literally inches from my face and still flapping severely. I thought it would be just a matter of time before I'd have to concede defeat and wrap the entire tent around me like a bivvy bag, and just wait out the storm til morning. I wasn't beaten just yet though. I needed to assess the situation beyond the tent inner and so I unzipped it as best I could, and peered through the misty air. I realised now why I was so wet. The guylines had indeed come free and the peg that held the main door closed had been wrenched out of the ground. The wind had forced the zip up and the door was wide open, allowing every drop of rain to lash against the inner, drenching it through. I knew there was no way I could get the tent back to its original sturdy position in weather like this, and so I had to make some decisions, decisions that would keep me safe for the next few hours, at least until the rain had stopped, or it had begun to get light.

My first logical thought process began. It was highly unlikely that I was in any serious danger. I wasn't camped near any trees that could fall on me, I wasn't going to drown, or get hypothermia with the temperatures still being relatively high, and I was pretty sure that, despite the intensity of the wind gusts, I wasn't going to be blown away. So, the worst case scenario in my view, was that I was just going to be drenched to the bone, with the possibility that some of my gear could be damaged or beyond repair and need replacing. When I'd come to this conclusion, I felt a small sense of relief, although it didn't stop the worry about the possible outcome. I didn't want to have to replace anything and I knew it would be very uncomfortable to be soaking wet for the rest of the night.

I formed a plan. The first step was to zip up the main door, and I reached into the rainy darkness to attempt this, several times, but the power of the wind continually pushed the zip back open. As I looked beyond the headtorch beam, I gazed upon my trekking pole, which I always kept just outside in the porch area. Grabbing it swiftly, I extended it to the height of my tent and thrust it against the poles as a brace, and then with all the strength I could muster, I forced the poles back into position. I placed the trekking pole at a forty-five degree angle to prevent the tent poles from collapsing once again and fixed it in position by my side. This was a good start, but now the outer fly sheet was thrashing around due to its' opened door and was letting rain in even more. Luckily, a peg that had come free was laying on the ground in the porch and with one hand I was able to grab the flailing door and peg it into the ground next to me, so at least it would provide a small amount of shelter.

I'd like to say that all was well after that and I slept soundly for the rest of the night, but having to hold the trekking pole firmly against each driving gust of wind whilst the rain seeped in through every available gap in the canvas, well, it was a long and exhausting night.

The rains finally ceased around 5am and as the sun peered apologetically over the horizon about an hour or so later, I knew the worst was behind me. I drifted in and out of slumber for the next couple of hours, woken each time the wind picked up and rattled the battered tent poles. I wasn't keen to get up, knowing that I would have to assess the damage and make some decisions about the day ahead, but I took the plunge around 8am and zipped open my sleeping bag.

The floor of my tent was filled with an inch of water and everything was completely saturated. My sleeping bag was so wet, I spent ten minutes wringing it out. My pillow, sleeping mat, backpack and several items of clothing, including my shoes, were drenched through. The only things that had stayed dry, were smaller items that I'd placed in an inner pocket within the tent, but on the whole, it was a dispiriting situation to be in. After checking the condition of my tent, I was grateful that the only thing wrong was a slightly bent pole and that it wouldn't prevent any further nights camping. For that, I was grateful. There was only one option for me though, to book accommodation for the coming night and dry everything out.

It was with great relief that I was so close to the city of Plymouth, which made it so much easier to find a bed and breakfast. I booked a room for two nights, with the idea that a full day off trail would give me time to get to a launderette and wash all my clothes and my sleeping bag. I decided that walking into Plymouth would be a chore, being drenched to the bone and still cold from the bracing winds of the morning didn't appeal to me in the slightest, and so I headed inland to Noss Mayo and onward to Newton Ferrers to catch a taxi.

Before leaving the brisk winds of the coast, the trail passed close to a small brick building, overlooking the sea at Gunrow's Down. I'd seen it from a distance as I pitched up the afternoon before, but I'd tried to keep out of sight from it, thinking that it may be inhabited. To my despair, it was an empty shell, that would have protected me greatly from the nights storm and prevented me from having to book extra nights in accommodation. Deflated by the discovery, I marched on, drying slowly in the ever-gusting breeze.

AUGUST 26TH

After a cosy night in the bed and breakfast, watching Pulp Fiction and ordering in a large, spicy, meat feast pizza, I took a gentle stroll towards Plymouth City Centre. It was a lovely, warm morning and I walked with purpose, carrying a full pack of dirty, wet clothes and my sleeping bag, to a launderette I'd pinpointed the evening before on the internet. Not only did I intend on cleaning all these items, but I decided to replace my shoes, purchasing new ones at a local outdoor shop. The shoes I wore were giving me a lot of pain in my toes and I deduced that they must be too small for me. I'd read before setting out on the trail that peoples' feet grow at least one size during a thru-hike. I guess the constant use and carrying so much weight was to blame, so I wasn't surprised to hear the kind lady in the store confirm that the footwear I had on, was indeed a size below what I should be wearing. After extensive searching, measuring, trying on and walking around the store in several pairs of trail shoes from several manufacturers, I picked a pair of Merrells. They had been my go-to brand for a number of years and so the decision wasn't difficult for me. The new ones were slightly different from shoes I'd had before, however, as they were more like a training shoe with soft uppers rather than hard, moulded rubber as I'd been accustomed to previously. They felt great and I couldn't wait to get back on the trail to try them out.

After a few hours of shopping, laundering and sending gear I wasn't using back home, I arrived at the bed and breakfast for my final night, happy in the knowledge that I would be over the border and taking my first steps in Cornwall the following day.

I had come up with a plan to make my tent a little more rigid, after the previous nights violent storm nearly damaged it. It was clear to me that the problem was with the tent poles and the fly sheet not holding together well during the high winds. This was supposed to be done with the positioning of four velcro straps, half way up the poles, but the velcro was so long, that it didn't fit snugly around the pole and allowed quite a bit of movement. My invention was a game-changer and one that still works perfectly to this day. I bought myself a sewing kit and a set of shoe laces. By stitching up the velcro, this made a loop, through which I threaded the shoe laces, one to be attached to each pole, and tied with a firm knot. Every time I would pitch my tent in future, instead of wrapping the velcro around the poles, I would tie the shoelace around in a simple bow. The lace was sufficiently coarse, that it offered plenty of grip and wouldn't slip or come undone, even in wet weather. To say I was proud of myself is an understatement and I've often considered writing to Alps Mountaineering, to tell them of my night of misery due to their manufacturing incompetence! I can't condemn them too harshly, apart from that, the tent has been the best I've ever used and don't regret the purchase for one second.

CORNWALL

AUGUST 27TH

Taking a couple of well-earned days off and heading out into the great unknown with freshly laundered clothes is a real motivation booster. Despite the weather being on the miserable side and knowing that I had a mile or two to walk through the urban sprawl of Plymouth before catching a ferry to a new county, I was surprisingly upbeat. As I plodded through the concrete jungle in my new shoes, my pack felt heavier than it had done in a long time, being filled to the brim with food and water for the coming days. But I didn't mind. New pastures lay ahead and I was very excited to begin these new adventures as soon as possible.

Being extra careful of approaching vehicles at each road crossing (which moved faster than anything I had seen for quite some time), the normality of impatient life had returned for a brief period and I was on full alert, but I was astounded by how much my mindset had changed over the past days, astounded at how easy life can actually be when there are no time restraints other than the setting and rising sun. Of course, I had a date in mind for when I wanted to finish the trail, and to achieve this, I would have to set my own time limits for mileage each day, making sure I was awake early enough to get these miles done to be able to reach my desired camping spot or accommodation, but if I didn't finish on the day I originally planned, it wouldn't be a problem. There was no urgency really. The only impatience I felt at this time was in the desire to return to the more relaxed way of life on that shallow ribbon of earth, where once more I'd feel the pressures of society drain from my body and I would again be at one with myself and nature......and seeing the first signs for the Cremyll ferry filled me with elation.

I took my first steps into Cornwall late morning. Mount Edgcumbe Country Park is a pleasant introduction to the county and a far cry from the neglected city across the water. A leafy path led me in the wrong direction past a duck pond. The coast path wasn't well signposted at that point, or maybe I was so happy to be back into the solitude and greenery that I didn't pay close enough attention. Either way, my mistake was corrected swiftly without complication and my journey continued in a pleasant weather window toward the tiny village of Kingsand. This brief moment of blue sky was to be briefer than I expected and as I approached the village, the heavens opened. From what felt like a return to summer after alighting the ferry, suddenly became monsoon-like. Thankfully, the narrow streets and high-sided buildings shielded me slightly from the high winds and diagonal rain that swept over the sea walls and I ducked into a small, elegantly furnished pub called the Halfway House Inn for a bite to eat and to wait for better weather. I would love to say that I sat in the pub long enough to dry out completely, but the service was so efficient and the food so tasty, that I was back into the terrible weather in less than thirty minutes.

After another thirty minutes of sheltering from the torrential rain under broad-limbed oak trees, things improved considerably. The sun shone in a clear blue sky and the summer warmth returned, it was truly becoming a wonderful day. With my stomach filled with good old English fish and chips, I'm sure I sauntered with a half smile for an hour or two, content at my life choices. Even a section of road walking towards the village of Freathy was not going to wipe the grin off my face, or so I thought.

I happened upon a large digger in the middle of the road. It was scooping chocolate-brown sludge from the street and dumping it on the verge. There had clearly been some kind of landslip due to the heavy rains over the previous days and the road was completely submerged in mud. I approached cautiously and spoke to a couple of guys in hi-viz jackets, that I assumed were over-seeing the excavations. Joking in tone but quite serious, I enquired "Is it safe?". I'm not sure I even waited for their reply as I continued towards the digger, and I really didn't assess the situation well.

The road was on a slight gradient and the lowest point was exactly where the digger was dispensing it's muck....and the exact point where me and my brand new shoes were heading! Thinking about the experience afterwards, I can now clearly remember the guy in the digger powering down the machine as I walked past, probably wondering why I chose my direction so poorly, knowing that inevitable chaos would ensue...and it did. My first steps into the tan abyss alerted me instantly to the fact that this was not going to end well, but my balance carried me onward, and even though my trekking pole reached out in desperation to prevent this forward motion, I had no choice but to stride into the unknown, swiftly lifting each foot out of the deepening mire like a frightened fawn, hoping that eventually I would step upon firm, dry concrete once more. It was about ten feet and ten seconds of panic later when I was able to turn around and see smiling faces of the workmen watching me. I'm sure they would have been desperately hoping to see me slip and face-plant in sloppy mud, something they would have laughed about in the site office canteen for years to come, but thankfully I had made it safely. My new shoes however, did not. I laughed it off of course and continued on my way, but inside I was enraged, at myself more than anything, for being so stupid. To this day, despite washing and being soaked by rain, the shoes still bear the scars, permanently discoloured.

I came across a rather deep puddle of rain water in a grassy field and decided the best course of action would be to completely drench my feet in it and scrub the sludge off my shoes. It took a good part of ten minutes and several clumps of long grass to be rid of the mud, but that only contributed to a new problem, wet feet. There was no point in changing my socks as a new pair would have been saturated within minutes, and the sun, albeit warm, would never have been warm *enough* to dry my shoes sufficiently, and so I pushed on, hoping that the warmth from my over-worked feet would assist in the drying process. Having wet feet is never a good thing while hiking long distances and having thoroughly soaked feet is even worse. By the end of the day I could feel blisters beginning to form near my inner heel bone. Normally, I would have stopped right away to attend to such medical matters once I'd felt any hotspot or irregularity, but I deduced that putting any kind of plaster over a newly forming blister in drenched socks would not have worked, and I didn't have any bandages to strap the heel. After pitching my tent in a field of inquisitive sheep next to a golf course later that evening, I was finally able to address the issue. Putting on dry socks had never felt so good, but I knew that the blister issue would remain for the coming days.

AUGUST 28TH

The following morning was an early start. I wasn't pitched on the golf club's land, but I was close enough to be awakened by a young, burly fellow mowing grass on the other side of a large hedgerow. I realised that I could be seen quite easily if I stood tall and so I thought it best to pack my tent away with a stoop.

The morning hours were quite uneventful, the weather pleasant yet overcast and quite typical of a British dawn. I pressed on casually through the quiet villages of Portwrinkle, Downderry and Seaton, stopping only once to restock my water supplies and buy a few extra snacks. I was planning a lunch stop in the larger village of Looe further along the coast. It was a place a friend of mine often frequents and so I was quite eager to see what all the fuss was about.

I descended a rather steep lane with white stone cottages and onto a thoroughfare which headed directly toward the village's main shopping street. It was a fairly peaceful walk with only a handful of people milling about and so I was not expecting the pandemonium when I arrived at the junction of the main boulevard. I was instantly bustled along by a wave of tourists. It was obvious that they were all visitors to the area, as I'm sure that no local in their right mind would ever consider joining this melee. It was somewhere I certainly didn't want to be and I weaved my way through the congestion as fast as I could possibly go. The experience wasn't to end once I'd exited the huddle of wayfarers though, the coast path out of the village towards Hannafore was shared with fast moving traffic and I was almost hit by a number of vehicles until the roadway widened half a mile further on. It is safe to say it would have taken wild horses to drag me into a Looe pub for lunch that day. I was quite happy to consume Snickers for the rest of the afternoon and head off into less crowded locations.

The coast path is very pretty between Hannafore and Talland Bay. It's very rocky in places and attention is required to prevent injuries, but it made for a lovely couple of hours in warm sunshine. There was also very few people around now that I had travelled a sufficient distance from Looe, quite welcomed I can assure you. Having missed my pub lunch window earlier, I came across the lovely beachside Talland Bay Cafe. It was devoid of crowds and so it was a relatively simple decision to take a short break and enjoy a refreshing pint of beer while absorbing the wonderful views of the cove. The trail that lay ahead was also quite spectacular and I was overwhelmed to have incredible views all the way to the Lizard, seventy five miles further to the south west. The late afternoon sun was warming, but there was a change on the horizon.

I had checked the weather radar on my phone earlier and it looked like there was a cold front moving in around 5.30pm, with the chance of heavy showers and strong winds. I'd pinpointed a spot on my map with good camping potential, but it was still quite a distance away and time seemed to be moving fast. Maybe the cafe break wasn't such a good idea after all?! All I could do was keep moving and hope that everything would turn out fine, as I'd done on countless occasions before. As I climbed the rocky path, past a peppering of Sea Thrift and gorse bush, the cloud seemed to be holding back, but I couldn't take any chances by stopping for too long, as the surrounding flora didn't provide any space on which to pitch my tent, however small it was. Not to mention it was all on a relatively steep slope. Thankfully, my hopes were answered as I descended into West Coombe. What looked on the map like a very hilly section of trail, turned out to be one of the best camping spots of the entire trip. There was a ribbon of flat ground, with grass so short that it could well have been used as a bowling green. There was even a bench overlooking the sea and it was clear that I wasn't the first to be considering staying here for the night, as there was a firepit surrounded by small rocks. It was perfect and I came across it just at the right time. Within five minutes of throwing down my pack, the clouds had gathered to the west and as quick as they had peered over the ridge beside the valley, they were bearing down on me with vengeance. Luckily, I had already taken out my tent from its stuff sack and was preparing the poles when the first spots of rain fell upon me. By the time the skies opened and poured it's fury upon me, I was safely inside my canvas home. The wind rumbled across the hill tops all night and the sea crashed violently upon the rocks, but the strange thing is, my tent didn't even flutter, and I slept like a baby.

AUGUST 29TH

An early start the following morning meant catching the ferry and reaching the shores of Fowey as the village was just waking up. It was an opportunity to experience the whole harbour bursting to life and I sat on a bench soaking it all up. I was high above the waterline and the warm sun beamed against my content cheeks. Watching canoeists and paddle boarders enjoying the gentle, ebbing tide, I didn't move for nearly an hour. It was during this time that I was approached by a local dog walker. Seeing my pack beside me, he enquired about my mission and we talked for a good ten minutes about the trail and the local area, before the conversation turned to where he and his family hailed from. Bizarrely, they were all brought up in the same town I now resided, some two hundred plus miles away in the East Midlands. As he mentioned towns and villages local to me, I nodded, knowing everywhere he talked about intimately. It's a small world after all, and it's these kinds of interactions that made this entire journey such a wonderful experience.

Polkerris is a lovely village, tucked away in a corner of St Austell Bay, surrounded by high woodland banks and

120

a cute little harbour wall. It offered a feeling of protection and was really quite cosy. It was probably one of my favourite villages along the Cornish coast and I was happy to find a small table on a pub veranda, where I munched on a large burger and chips and washed it all down with a couple of pints of beer.

Before I could finish my tasty meal however, it began to rain. There was no shelter on the decking and with the pub being full of people, I had no option but to sit out the downpour. Enter, my trusty umbrella! I must have looked like a complete weirdo, sitting on my own in a heavy shower of rain under an umbrella, eating a soggy meal. The table top had slats of wood, which were separated by gaps, giving me enough room to slide my umbrella handle into and wedging it sufficiently so that the blustery winds would not whisk it away along the beach.

Cowering, with my face just a few inches from my plate, I was determined that this brief interruption would not get the better of me, and I finished my food at the amusement of the young waitress, sheltering behind the glass doors of the pub bar. I found the situation quite funny too and gave her a quick smile and a wink as I continued merrily on my way, slightly intoxicated after the two strong beers.

The trail took me past yet another beach and yet another holiday park. I was very grateful for this this time, as the burger and chips were weighing heavy on my stomach and the beers had gone through me like an injection of Sauerkraut. A car park provided me with a convenient toilet block, and despite having to dig deep for a twenty pence coin to get me inside, it was a relief to find somewhere so soon after the first belly gurglings occurred.

It wasn't often that I used these kinds of toilets and as I entered I was taken aback by how technologically advanced it was, compared to the last one I'd frequented. The cubicle was illuminated by a bright green light on the inside of the door. I was curious about this, but so desperate to concentrate on the reason I'd entered the room that I initially dismissed it's purpose.

After attending to business, flushing and washing hands with only a swipe of my palm across a sensor to produce soap, water and a dryer from the same nozzle, I turned towards the door to head out into the fresh, afternoon air. I realised there was another sensor pad on the door itself and concluded that this is what I must press to exit the lavatory. On doing so, however, the green light that so beautifully lit the loo with a relaxing ambience, turned instantly red, and a mechanism within the door slammed worryingly loud. It was now locked, and the menacing hue that bounced off the polished stone walls sent a shiver of panic through me. As the confusion subsided, it then occurred to me that the door had been open the entire length of my stay, and I'm sure my cheeks warmed with embarrassment (and the same red glow as the locked door) as I swiftly departed. Maybe digging holes and crapping behind trees is actually the safer option?!

The trail ahead would take me through a section of the coast I was not particularly looking forward to, St. Austell. I hadn't been there for many years, and I certainly hadn't hiked the coast path in that area before, but there was something in the back of my mind that told me it wasn't going to be very pleasant, and the instructions from the hikers I met on Golden Cap all those days before, telling me of a diversion around the area, were also playing on my mind. I was clearly hiking on the fringe a built-up area as I passed factories and railway lines, hotels and another golf course. The amount of people on the trail had increased significantly and I even passed groups of younger folk, enjoying the warm, early evening with portable barbeques and cans of beer. It was a bank holiday weekend and maybe that was why I was a little uneasy about heading towards a larger town on a bustling friday night. Although I was forced to walk through decaying suburbs for a brief amount of time, I soon reached a tiny harbour at Charlestown. For such a small inlet, it was heaving with pub goers and tourists and my instinct was to push on a swiftly as I could.

As I climbed a narrow concrete pathway out of the harbour, I glanced up. Ahead of me was a metal gate, and it was padlocked shut. On it a sign, telling of fines for anyone passing through this section, as it was dangerous due to a landslip. This was the diversion the hikers warned me of and a diversion I should ignore if I didn't want an extra few miles walk adding to the days' total. I remember them telling me that there was enough room under the gate to squeeze myself and my pack and continue on the coast path, which in their eyes, was safe enough to walk along. What I now remembered clearly, is that their packs were quite a bit smaller than mine, but not being deterred, I thrust it into the dust and forced it through to the other side. The gates, not being completely secured, rattled violently as I crawled through the narrow gap and I was acutely aware of the noise I was making, and the fact the people sitting outside the pub at the bottom of the hill would have no doubt heard the commotion easily. I scurried into the woodlands like a frightened rabbit and continued along the path, which tapered to a precarious few inches at certain points, but, as the hikers had told me, was safe enough. The process had to be repeated in reverse when I reached the opposite end of the diversion, but again I was able to squeeze myself and my pack under the locked gate and save myself the extra miles, and the embarrassment of having to go back past the pub.

AUGUST 30TH

After a peaceful night camping on the edge of a corn field, I arrived at Pentewan Beach quite early in the day. It was time to do some washing and have a proper breakfast, and so I found a lovely, flat area of grass next to a holiday park and exploded my pack. Socks, t-shirts and underwear were priority as I was down to one pair of each, and even they had a couple of days wear. Tossing a gel packet into my water-filled ziploc bag, I frantically scrubbed my clothes, and watched the clear water turn to a frothy beige in a matter of seconds. Next, the wringing out of the water. Not my favourite bit at all, but at least my hands smelled fresh and clean afterwards too.

A couple of peaceful hours passed and as the park dwellers emerged to walk their excited dogs upon the sands, I sat amidst soggy attire, dangling from my pack and the fence behind me, eating a gourmet meal of porridge oats, powdered milk and banana flavoured whey protein powder. It was actually quite nice and along with a coffee, made for a welcomed meal and a relaxing morning staring out to sea. I took a very steady walk towards Mevagissey, over undulating grassy fields with excellent views of St Austell Bay. At one point, and to the amazement of passing day hikers, I decided to lay out my damp clothes upon a hill top to finish the drying process, and also to air my tent in the warm cliff top breeze. After only an hour, everything was dry and I re-packed it all with precision in stuff sacks and stored them neatly in my pack.

Arriving in Mevagissey just after noon on a bank holiday sunday, I was expecting the same hell I faced when entering Looe. It couldn't have been more different. Of course, there were many people milling through the tight streets and along the harbour walls, but it was a complete contrast to the previous experience. There was an air of relaxation, a bustle but with a sense of acceptance, like everyone was totally aware of others' personal space and even welcomed it. I cruised past pasty shops and ice cream parlours with souvenirs hanging from doorways and window frames. The aroma of fresh baking hung in the street and draped itself like a tempting devil upon my shoulders. It won. My guts bubbled in anticipation of food and the lure of The Ship Inn was too great. I was offered a cosy table in a corner of the bar area and I ordered a plate of burger and chips for the second day running. This one though, exceeded the previous days' by some margin, and if it hadn't have been for a queue of people outside, all desperately hoping for a table, I may have ordered a second helping. I was sitting alone on a table large enough for four and I noticed the waitress look my way a couple of times, longing for me to move on and free up the space. If the service hadn't have been so good, I may have been vindictive and extended my stay with another pint of beer and a dessert, but I happily obliged. As I lifted my pack onto my shoulders I noticed a large pool of grease on the floor where I had sat. Awkwardly, I headed for the door before the waitress could look my way again and realise I'd completely missed my plate while eating my burger, causing a slippery mess. Or maybe she had seen me eating like a two-year-old and that was why she was giving me looks of disdain earlier. I will never know.

Along a pleasant section of trail past Chapel Point, I saw the most desirable house in the most idyllic location thus far on my trek. A grand, five bedroom residence with a stunning twelve acres of land surrounding it, and a wonderful sea view, valued at a mere three million pounds! Yes, I did my homework on it later, it was that fascinating. In jealousy, I huffed past, on well maintained gravel tracks that even the sheep looked proud to be walking on, towards Gorran Haven and my camp spot of choice for the night at Dodman Point.

Dodman Point is the highest headland on the South Cornwall coast. It's the site of an Iron Age fort and there stands a huge granite cross. It's also a great place to camp. Slightly up the bank away from the main coast path, it offers stunning views directly out to sea, where I watched fishing boats trawl the sea floor for hours, until the still evening brought the most spectacular moon rise. It was one of the most relaxing evenings so far and despite taking many photos of the serene panorama under the intense glow of the moon, none of them did it justice. I guess it was just one of those moments that you had to see with your own eyes to know exactly how beautiful it was. No words could ever describe the feeling I had that night, but I know I didn't want to be anywhere else.

AUGUST 31ST

Undulating cliff tops to the south of Penare would present a bit of fun on a sunny monday morning. As I descended a heather and gorse-filled slope, I came face to face with a few wild ponies. I'd seen many on occasion before, and even had to step to one side while a string of them walked past me on a narrow section of trail, but these were happily munching on the undergrowth along the path and wouldn't move an inch for me. There was no way around and I was unsure what to do. There were no other paths that I could take to avoid them, it was the coast path and that was it. I tried yelling at them and I tried running quickly towards them, but all in vain. I was in no rush and would have taken a break to give them time to disperse of their own accord, if it wasn't for another pony closing in behind me. I was now completely trapped.

I looked at the prickly gorse on each side of me. There was no way through it without scratching my legs til they bled and probably ripping my trousers to shreds, and I was not going to be doing that. I'd climb onto the back and ride a pony out of there before attempting that. As my mind raced to reach an answer to the situation, for some reason I remembered a comment on a youtube video I'd seen a couple of months before, about a guy walking the Pacific Crest

Trail and being confronted by a pack of wild dogs. He'd said that opening his trekking umbrella had scared the dogs and had saved him from a serious attack.

Genius I thought, and so, brolly in hand, I approached the pony blocking the descent, giving it at least one more chance to move and let me pass, but it wasn't to be. Operation Umbrella was unleashed. With one swift thrust, I forced the brolly open as fast as I could, hoping that the wide, silver surface would scare the pony into submission. Well, it did that alright! I've never seen an animal move so fast in my entire life. Before I could even close the brolly again, the pony and all of his friends were sprinting down the side of the hill. It wasn't nice to scare them of course, but they'd backed me into a corner, and I had to come out fighting....well, flapping!

I passed the stunning Caerhays Castle in beautiful warm sunshine. It was the setting for the film 'Miss Peregrine's home for peculiar children' and is situated in 120 acres of lush gardens and woodland, and it's a very pleasant walk along that section of coast path. I took an extended break overlooking Long Point and Perbean Beach, watched a number of people swimming in the clear blue ocean and kayakers heading out to sea from Porthluney Cove. It was a glorious morning and I even decided to put my shorts on, to soak up the warming rays of the sun.

Just over the rolling hills, nestled in a charming cove, was West Portholland. It was the birthplace and childhood home of a friend and I took a short, half mile detour inland to visit the property, and take a photo for him. It probably hadn't changed a great deal, I thought. A beautiful white-washed stone cottage in an idyllic location, quiet and undisturbed. Half-expecting to be moved on by the current owners, as they emerged shortly after taking pictorial evidence of my visit, I turned back for the coast.

The rugged coastline between Portholland and Nare Head was spectacular. Hugging cliff tops for miles, the narrow footpath, lined with sea thrift and gorse blowing gently in the warm breeze, was invigorating. With the sun now high in the sky, the sweat began to pour as I ascended the precipitous headlands, and I took many breaks to admire the splendour and consume much needed food and water.

Reaching Nare Head in the afternoon, the trail turned north for a while and the sun shimmered on the surface of the water across Gerrans Bay. There was a fantastic view of Portscatho across the bay and somewhere in that direction was my camp site for the night.

I arrived at Pendwower Beach around 4pm and after taking my eye off the trail signs temporarily, realised I'd taken a wrong turn after walking for quite some time up a steep road. I continued to the top of the hill in the knowledge that I'd simply be able to turn left and return to the beach on another route. While this was indeed possible, there seemed to be a lot more traffic, and the road was particularly narrow at some points, meaning I would have to step aside into the undergrowth to allow the vehicles past.

One car had me cursing my decision to choose this road. He had driven slowly, and cautiously, past me, even though at that point there was plenty of room and I didn't even have to move out of his way. What followed was simply laughable, although initially I was getting quite frustrated.

A large queue of cars had appeared, all waiting to come up the hill, and with no room for anyone to turn, it was up to the car that had driven so carefully past me minutes earlier, to reverse back to the top of the road to provide everyone with enough space to pass. Well, I've never seen anyone reverse a car so poorly. From left to right he weaved, clipping hedgerows and having to drive forward again to straighten up. He couldn't manage five yards before heading off road. I stood there for quite some time, gobsmacked by what I was witnessing. 'How did this guy pass a driving test?', I thought. I was stood next to a small turning for a house, a space that was ample for a car to pull into, giving room for others to pass. I even gestured to the driver that he had space to reverse into, but he continued past me, inching backwards and driving forwards again for easily five minutes. I was scared to move from the space I'd found myself, knowing that I had a quick access point over a metal gate if needed, and for a brief moment, I thought I may need it.

I think the drivers waiting to move on were getting a little annoyed at this stage, but my feelings of anger and impatience faded fast and were replaced by amazement and joviality, in equal measure. I decided I wasn't going to wait any longer and with a wry smile, started to walk past the ever-increasing queue of vehicles. I could see faces of disbelief peer at me through the windscreens, some with scowls towards the other car, some were even shaking their heads and rolling their eyes. It was a complete farce, and I'd love to know how long it took them to move on, but I had places to be and apart from the odd glance back up the hill to see the struggle continue, I carried on towards the beach to correct my earlier mistake.

Reaching a village store before its closing time was always a challenge after 5pm. Some closed ridiculously early, even at the weekends, so I was overjoyed to find one in Portscatho with just two minutes to spare before they locked up. I'd booked a bed and breakfast in Falmouth for the following day, and so I didn't need a lot of extra food, but a few pies and some chocolate bars for the relatively short walk the next morning was ample. The cosy coastal village was heaving with people. Pubs spilling out onto the streets and blaring music made me feel a little uncomfortable, but I was soon heading to the coast path once again.

Time was against me and I was still unsure as to where I would be laying my head, but a corn field overlooking Greeb Point provided the solution. I had to be quite stealthy with my pitch. At the top of the field, no more than fifty feet away, was a track, that looked like it had seen vehicles in the recent days. I took the chance to pitch up, constantly aware of noises I might make and noises that would indicate people walking down the track. There was a hawthorn hedgerow sheltering me from the prevailing southwesterly winds, but standing at around five feet high, it didn't provide much cover from prying eyes, and I may have been easily spotted from a nearby house.

I watched the house for quite a while, assessing the situation like a sniper would eyeball his enemy. I saw no movement at all. There were no lights on, no vehicles in the driveway, nothing. The sun disappeared over the horizon and the light faded fast, but still no light from any part of the house. Curiosity got the better of me and I decided to do an internet search about the property. I had seen the name of it on the map and it instantly came up in the search list. Clicking onto a website, I was relieved to find out that it was a holiday destination, a selection of cottages for rent and also equipped to offer wedding functions. It was clear from that moment on, that even if people renting the property were to walk past me, they would have no authority to evict me from my location. I felt a little more comfortable about the whole situation and slept quite calmly. It was a peaceful night after all.

SEPTEMBER 1ST

There was really no panic the next morning. I wasn't too far from the ferry crossings that would take me across the bay to Falmouth and so I enjoyed the morning sun and had several breaks around St. Anthony Head, a very pretty, but very exposed peninsula. It offered wonderful panoramic views across the water to the bustling town, and the coastline to the north was almost tropical in appearance. It was quite clear that the Gulf Stream had major influence in this area.

Looking at the ferry times, I had to do a spot of planning. I'd have to catch two boats, one to St. Mawes and then one to Falmouth. I'd ambled around St Anthony Head for long enough and the afternoon was suddenly upon me, and so I made the decision to catch the ferries as soon as possible, and spend any extra time I had, before being allowed into the Bed and Breakfast, to walk around the town itself.

My phone battery was running very low by this point and I had no more charge left in my powerbank. A quick charge in the pub in Mevagissey was all I'd had since Plymouth. This wasn't a worry to begin with, seeing as I'd be in Falmouth very soon and able to charge everything up, but as I arrived at the Place Ferry crossing, panic set in when I read a sign that said the ferry wasn't running. It would be a days walk at least, just getting across the bay to St. Mawes and without my phone, I would be doing it blind, no bus times or taxi numbers, should I need them. I wouldn't even be able to plan a route to walk without my phone, and I wouldnt make my accommodation...which I'd already paid for.

I'd considered buying paper maps before I started the trip, to assist me in the likelihood that I'd run out of battery power, but after calculating the cost and the weight of the several maps needed to cover the entire trail, it just wasn't feasible. I purchased a subscription to online Ordnance Survey maps instead, which gave me full access to the entire British Isles and enabled me to screenshot each step of the trail for the upcoming days, should my internet signal drop out. This didn't help at all if my phone battery died of course, but it was a risk worth taking, so I thought. So to be in a position where I may have to walk an unexpected and extended detour inland without any assistance from maps, was quite frustrating.

By chance, just before I set off to begin my long, frustrating afternoon of getting lost, I noticed a couple of guys stumbling across the muddy banks of the estuary. I'm not entirely sure why, but I decided to stumble over the mud myself, to ask the guys about the ferry, and I'm so pleased I did. My panic immediately eased when they told me it *was* running and would be along very shortly, as soon as the tide had risen a few more inches. I was so close to leaving the area, and I would have missed the ferry arriving just ten minutes later if those guys hadn't have been there, or if I hadn't have seen them. It was a moment of pure luck that I felt I'd earned and which led to a lovely afternoon in Falmouth, sitting on the dock side in warm sunshine, watching boats go by and enjoying a plate of chips. Although at times, I feared they'd be stolen from me by the countless number of Herring Gulls circling above.

The Prince of Wales pub was a conveniently situated bed and breakfast, right on the harbour and overlooking the main shopping street through the town. The post office and several food stores being close by, I was able to do a few chores, including sending some unused gear back home to cut my weight even further, stocking up on new ziploc bags and clothes washing items and treating myself to a very continental evening meal, which incorporated a huge bowl of black olives, some crusty bread and a bottle of Merlot. The room was pleasant, with a comfortable double bed and despite the lack of effort needed to arrive in Falmouth that day, it was the first mattress I'd slept on in many days and as such, it wasn't long before I was asleep. The bottle of wine may have had something to do with it also!

SEPTEMBER 2ND

The following morning was a slight blur as I headed down to the pub bar for my breakfast, head throbbing a little from my wine intake the previous evening. A beautifully cooked full English awaited me, with freshly-squeezed orange juice and a strong cup of coffee. Much needed, but a bit of a struggle to finish with churning guts. I was hoping to hit the trail much earlier than I did, but feeling a little rough, I dropped my key on the bar with only a couple of minutes to spare before my checkout time.

It was to be a momentous day on the trail. I would be passing the half way point at Porthallow, and to get there, taking my last ferry crossing of the south coast. After the near-fiasco of the previous day, not having to plan for ferry crossings was very much welcomed, and my irritation with them was confirmed when I arrived at the Helford River crossing and the tide was, once again, too low for any sailing.

After chatting with the ferryman, I was informed that it would be at least an hour before he could take me across, and that was going to be the very earliest that he'd risk it. Knowing that I was hiking the coast path, he enlightened me on another forthcoming problem, the next estuary around the coast, Gillan Creek. Once I'd been ferried across Helford River, I would have a limited amount of time to walk a distance of around three miles, to get to Gillan Creek before the tide had risen and forced me to walk an extra two miles inland around the estuary. The challenge was on!

Alighting the ferry at Helford Point, I wished the ferryman well and set off with purpose in each stride. As the trail hugged the estuary for a while, I could almost feel the eyes of everyone I'd just left across the water, watching intently, following my progress. I didn't want to disappoint, my head was down and I was on a mission. It was a shame that I had to walk so fast, as the trail was very pretty along that section of coast, from what I can remember of it. Gentle woodlands and quaint coves, eventually leading to a short stretch of roadway and down to the creek. It had taken me just short of one hour and the tide looked low enough to walk across the estuary.

The trail was not very well signed at this particular point. One sign indicating the creek crossing and another pointing down the road for the diversion, but I could see no marker on the other bank. I decided to give it a go, even though the water was rushing in fast and would very shortly be ankle deep. It looked to me like there were two areas of flowing water to navigate, with a raised sand bank separating them. The first crossing looked to be the deepest, but with several stones perfectly placed in the silty mud, I was able to reach the bank in the middle, albeit nervously. The second crossing was much more intense, with the water flowing much faster, and some of the rocks looking very slippery indeed. Some were submerged already and I feared that I was about to get very wet feet, but there was no turning back now, and I had to move fast. Using my trekking pole for stability, I took my first tentative steps, feeling the the water lap against the soles of my shoes and expecting to slip at any moment. But before I knew it, I was on the sand again and the only casualty was a splash of sea water on the bottom of my trousers.

Thinking I was home and dry, and feeling quite proud of myself, I looked towards the estuary bank for any sign of a trail marker, only to realise that I was not out of the woods just yet. I still had about fifty feet of soft ground to cover and I had no idea which direction I should be heading. My eyes fixed upon an old wooden sign, attached to what looked like a boat dock and assumed it must be the trail. I couldn't have been more wrong. The sign read 'No Trespassing' or 'No public access', something along those lines, I forget which. What I do remember is the panic I felt as I turned around to see the water rising fast behind me. If I didn't find my way out of this estuary soon, I would be swimming, that was for sure. There were a few boats beached in the soft sands and were awaiting their watery ticket to freedom, and I had visions of climbing aboard one of them and having to wait out the day, but with only a matter of minutes before things became quite desperate, I found my way out thirty feet further up the bank and I was delighted, and much relieved, to be back on trail.

It wasn't too long before I arrived in the sleepy village of Porthallow, and on the cove, in the middle of a shale beach, stood a tall, weathered, granite monument. To be honest, I wasn't sure if this was the trail half-way marker or not. I had to ask a kindly fellow, who was serving in the pub just a few feet from the shoreline. I'd entered the pub for obvious reasons, to celebrate the achievement of completing half the trail, but I had to enquire about the structure to know if it did actually represent the mid-point. There were many words etched into the stone, but none to suggest I'd just walked half way round the longest trail in England, and I was a little disappointed to say the least.

I sat with my beer in the increasingly windy conditions, peering over a wall at the monument with a frown. My ignorance for what was etched on the slab was clearly due to lack of research before my arrival, but I have since learned that this intriguing collection of words and phrases were gathered especially by the local community and entitled 'Fading Voices', and celebrates the coast path and its spiritual benefits. Still, I was a little annoyed by it at the time. If this was indeed erected to represent a huge achievement for many hikers, why was there not some recognition of this? It wasn't until I returned home, that I found out the stone was engraved on the other side too! An extra five feet of walking to investigate the rear of the structure, would have revealed the words I'd been so keen to view. There's some irony in that, I'm sure!

The trail deviated inland for several miles with a fair bit of road walking, before a brief glimpse of the coast at the tiny hamlet of Porthoustock and then inland again to the quaint Rosenithon, where for a brief moment I got lost, completely missing the signpost for the coast path turn off from the main street. I think I was distracted by the villages ambience, it was so peaceful and the houses were idyllic. I can get seriously frustrated with myself by missing trail markers and adding extra mileage to my day for not paying close enough attention, but on this occasion I didn't really mind, I was enjoying the scenery and the leisurely vibe of the area.

The atmosphere was soon to change as I approached the coast once more. The weather had been quite dreary all day, but I hadn't noticed it while walking inland. I'd been sheltered from the wind and I'd been distracted by views other than gorse and waves, so it was quite a shock to the system to be on an exposed section of headland, with no protection from the elements at all.

I'd entered a series of gravel pits and quarries. I was unsure whether they were still in use, but there were plenty of signs around warning to stay away from the rock faces and excavation works that had already been done. The trail was very rocky underfoot and harsh on the calves and there were no deviations off the trail for any respite, it was clearly marked, and I was forced from one gravelled road to another by signs and fences. There were areas that looked ideal for camping, flat and grassy, but were surrounded by earthworks and bunkers. To camp there just didn't feel right, but with the wind picking up and drizzle in the air, it was time to start thinking about my final location for the day.

As I turned to face the south west around Lowland Point, the wind increased ten-fold and the precipitation turned from a gentle patter to an aggressive combination of sea spray and driving rain. Even though it was only around 6pm, the failing light could have fooled me into thinking it was nearer sundown. I had to find somewhere to camp soon, but my first thoughts were to find somewhere sheltered for a while, to have a coffee and wait out the worst of the bad weather. My decision to do this would be the best idea I had all day.

I came across a small copse, with a compact area to sit which was sheltered from wind and rain. Compared to the ground beyond the trees, this was almost dry. I deemed it the perfect spot to have a long break and I immediately got my stove out to boil some water for a coffee. I took off my rain jacket and hung it up on one of the branches above me, in the hope that it would drip dry over the next hour or so. The rain had soaked through it completely and it was just as wet on the inside as out.

I must have sat for an hour, staring into the murk and wondering how long I would have to wait for the rain to ease enough so I could move on. I looked up at my jacket, flapping gently in the breeze. I then looked behind me.....then to my right.....then to my left.....Suddenly, like someone had switched on a lightbulb inside my mind, the realisation that this tiny nook I'd found amidst the trees might actually be large enough to squeeze my tiny one person tent into. This couldn't be right, surely? Why had I not come to this conclusion when I arrived here? I would have snapped up these kinds of places in a heartbeat on any given night since I started the trail.

I think I must have spent the next ten minutes scratching my head, wondering why I hadn't even considered pitching up in that spot. When I finally took the groundsheet out of my pack and laid it on the floor, I laughed so hard. It was a perfect fit. Within ten minutes I'd created myself a cosy little home for the night; no wind, no rain and out of sight from the trail. With the daylight fading fast, I settled in for the night, watching the wind whip the bushes upon the trail I had walked to get here. At one point I was startled by the sight of another hiker, walking away from me and towards the quarries, the rain lashing upon his backpack. He had no idea I was here and I smiled, glad that I wasn't in his situation anymore.

SEPTEMBER 3RD

The weather had only marginally improved by the morning. A thick clag hung over the area, but at least it had stopped raining. The air was still and silent and my senses were heightened, as every sound I made while packing up my tent, seemed to drift into the mist and echo eerily back to me. It was like I was in a horror movie and I imagined a mythical creature such as a werewolf, stalking me in the gloom. Of course, I am completely aware that these beasts do not actually exist, but I still turned around nervously with every rustle from nearby bushes, and listened intently for a few seconds to verify I was still alone.

I saw nothing or nobody else on the trail, in any bushes or in my vivid imagination, until I entered Coverack, even then, it was only one old man waiting for his daily newspaper at the local shop. I'd arrived nearly an hour too early to get the supplies I needed for the distance to Penzance. I wasn't sure whether to wait or make alternative plans for re-supply, but the old man standing patiently outside the shop, being very vocal and opinionated in his beliefs regarding issues of the day, made the decision much easier. I would head off-trail to the village of Lizard, just a couple of miles inland from the coast, then walk directly south to pick up the coast path once again at Lizard Point. I'd miss a few miles of coastal trail, but in the current weather conditions, I decided it wouldn't be too enjoyable anyway.

When I arrived in Lizard village late morning, it was actually a lot busier than I'd expected. Even as the rain began to fall, tourists were arriving in droves to make the short walk to England's most southerly point on the mainland. I knew it would be a major attraction during the summer months, but seeing the dedication to viewing this in such awful weather was a real eye-opener, and it just seemed to get worse with every minute that passed.

I was relieved to duck into a local store for some supplies and to escape the ever-worsening winds, only to find the shelves almost empty of anything worthy of calling food. It was the strangest shop I'd ever been in, with two aisles offering an eclectic mix of charcoal, baked beans and toilet roll, nothing of which was of any use to me, unless I was planning to re-enact a scene from Blazing Saddles! Thankfully, another shop provided me with the essentials I needed to see me through another couple of days.

I began to walk in the direction of Lizard Point, but after seeing the coastal attraction inundated with people, battered by stormy winds and horizontal rain, I decided that visiting this location would have to wait for another day. I turned north west, towards a bleak and unsheltered landscape. Rocky cliffs and wide expanses of flat grassland, all continually pummelled by the intense weather, with no end of either natural phenomenom in sight. I just had to get my head down and endure it.

It was an hour or two before the rain relented and I was able to put my coat hood down. It hadn't made too much difference anyway, the rain had soaked me through and I was cold and miserable, but there was a glimmer of hope in sight. A soft ray of sunlight warmed my face for the first time in more than a day and suddenly, I remembered why I was here. In less than an hour, the clouds had cleared, the wind had subsided and the ground began to dry beneath my feet in radiant beams of celestial glory.

I descended into a tiny, sheltered valley near Soap Rock. After miles of arduous hiking with my head down, unable to appreciate the beauty of the landscape, I chose to take a break and admire the surrounding hills with a well-earned cup of warm coffee. If it had have been later in the day, I probably would have opted to pitch for the night in that beautiful spot, but it was early afternoon and there were many people still hiking the trail. I sat for at least a couple of hours though; drying my clothes in the warm sun, daydreaming, reminiscing, planning the coming days....watching a herd of kamikaze cows attempt to graze upon the steepest of grass banks! I've seen dead sheep in ravines due to a fall from such a height, but I actually found it quite comical to imagine a cow do the same (although I'm glad they were safe, I was secretly hoping to see one fall!)

My afternoon break was finally disturbed by a helicopter hovering above me. It sparked a little paranoia, wondering if they were watching to make sure that I didn't camp there, even though it was only about 3pm. I had every intention to move on. With the clouds dispersed, I was sure to have at least five hours of daylight ahead of me and feeling revived by the glorious sunshine, I believed I could have walked another twelve miles. With my stride waning by the fifth mile, and the chopper continuing to circle the skies above me, I knew it was time to look for a camp spot. I even considered another bed and breakfast, and made a single phone call to a place in Mullion, but they were fully booked. The time was pressing on and it was a choice between sitting around phoning accommodation to find there was nothing available, or keep walking to find a good spot to pitch up. I chose the latter and I most certainly made the right decision.

In darkening skies, I circled Poldhu Cove, where many people were still surfing and enjoying a few beers upon the beach. It seems that daylight is not an issue in this part of the world! However, it was for me. I made one last steep climb on an overgrown side trail behind a creepy church, to appear on a stunning cliff top with amazing views of the setting sun. The grass was very long and quite spongy and made for a perfect mattress, it was the ultimate in comfort.

The helicopter that had been flying around the area all day (if it was the same one) continued into the late evening and I had to wear my headphones as earplugs to drown out the noise. By midnight I had awoken to complete silence and taken them off, but less than an hour later, the chopper returned, circling the cliff top in close proximity to my tent. I froze completely, baffled by its presence, but it didn't take me too long to come to the conclusion that they couldn't possibly be looking for me, or maybe I just didn't care anymore. I put my headphones back on in an attempt to drown out the incessant noise and attempted to sleep.

SEPTEMBER 4TH

I awoke early the following morning, to the calming sounds of the sea below the cliff tops and the odd gull cry overhead. I'd booked a bed and breakfast in Penzance for the coming evening and an early start was what I needed to complete the twenty mile trek to get there. It was a peaceful morning with a beautiful crimson sunrise and the lengthy walk along Porthleven Sands was breath-taking. I arrived in Porthleven village early enough to experience the first signs of life on another summers day on the coast. Dog walkers, shop staff preparing their businesses for the days' customers, rubbish collectors removing the previous days' trash from the bins and delivery drivers, reversing their large vehicles into loading bays while the streets were almost traffic-free. These were the best moments on trail for me. This was the essence of coastal village life and something I was quite envious of. I was sharing my favourite time of day with people that lived and breathed these amazing few moments, with the gulls, the sun and the continuous rumble of the comforting waves. In just a few short hours, the tranquillity would be replaced by the bustle of tourism and the constant purr of traffic.

I arrived in Marazion mid afternoon. It was oppressively humid and my forehead was dripping with sweat. Uncomfortable and hungry, I searched for a shop to buy a couple of snacks and a cold drink, to see me through til Penzance, just a few miles away. I entered a small convenience store that sold a few local gifts too, and I decided to have a quick browse while the queue at the till died down.

Remembering I had a small tear on one of the waist straps on my pack, I picked up a small, sew-on patch. A very nicely embroidered black and white Cornish flag. To this day, I have no idea where I lost it, but I never did see the patch again after that afternoon. I seem to recall putting it in my pack, but it simply vanished. Thankfully, it was only a quid!

While waiting to purchase the vanishing item, along with an ice cold can of Coke and a sausage roll, I stood behind a young mother, buying a stuffed animal for her daughter. I think it was a zebra, but I can't be certain, it may have been a unicorn! Whatever it was, it was held in high regard by the child and she was adamant that that was the gift she was wanting, despite her mother trying to talk her out of It....for at least five minutes. They were both at the counter and in the process of paying for a few items, when the mother decided to point out a larger stuffed toy on the shelves behind the shopkeeper. I lost count of the amount of times the child said 'No, I want this one', but each time she was urged to think about the other gift. Meanwhile, behind me, the queue in the shop was growing considerably and the last person was stood in the doorway, battling for space with each new customer that entered. The situation was getting very frustrating, not just for me, but for everyone behind too. I could see impatience growing on each face as the mother tried to redirect her daughter's attention away from the toy in her hands. I was nearly at a point where I was actually considering buying the other toy for her, just to please them both and get them out of the way so we could all continue with our day. It was infuriating to say the least.

Happy to be on my way, finally, I passed a few sand dunes before the road walk into Penzance and thought I'd take a break, drink my Coke and eat my sausage roll. I chose a relatively quiet section of the beach, where I could bask in the warming rays of the sun, bouncing off the shimmering waves. I had a perfectly relaxing few minutes, with just the monotonous sounds of continuous traffic from the road behind me, until a couple had the very impolite idea to sit directly in front of me, even though there was several acres of empty beach around. Blocking my wonderful view of the sea, they talked ceaselessly, completely ruining the ambience and raising my stress levels to a greater height than they were in the shop just ten minutes earlier. It was time to go before I exploded.

The traffic that had sounded so calming to me while I was sat upon the beach, now began to irritate. It was a long road walk to Penzance and the pavement was crowded with tourists and the roads filled with congestion. I could tell I was nearing a large town and there was no escape from the turmoil. From being in the perfect environment earlier in the day in Porthleven, this way a far cry from an enjoyable experience, but a hike along the coast was always going to involve very different surroundings and atmospheres, and I had to take the up's and down's with each stride.

I'd never been to Penzance before and even though there were areas of it that felt a little rough around the edges, on the whole it wasn't too bad at all. The room at the Warwick House bed and breakfast was compact and cosy, and run by a very likeable husband and wife team. It was situated perfectly, close to the seafront and not too far from amenities in the town centre. They also provided one of the best breakfasts I'd had on the trip so far, again, a full English (as most B&B's provide) but was cooked to absolute perfection and was served with a huge smile, in a lovely dining room.

SEPTEMBER 5TH

On a beautiful saturday morning, I took the opportunity to do a complete batch of laundry at a local launderette, setting me up for the following few days with fresh-smelling clothes, in what was to set be a very warm spell of weather. Land's End was the next big landmark to focus on and then i would be on the 'home straight', as it were, with the south coast completed and ahead of me, the rugged north coast of Cornwall, which I'd been very much looking forward to.

I was back on trail a little later than expected due to the laundry, and with the morning quickly disappearing, I set off at a pace along the main roads through Newlyn and Mousehole, to try and make up some time. Unfortunately, any progress I was hoping to make, was severely hampered by a number of runners heading in the same direction. The amount of runners seemed to grow rapidly within the hour and I was a little thrown off by it all, having to step aside to let them pass at regular intervals. Scratching my head with curiosity, I searched the internet to see what was going on, as all the runners were wearing numbers on their shirts, and this could only mean that it was an organised event. And sure it was: The Lizard Point to Land's End Classic Quarter. A 44 mile race around the south west coast path, and every one of these runners was set to encounter me at some stage, walking in the same direction and getting in their way. It was clear from that moment on that I was not going to make the progress I'd hoped, I wouldn't be able to listen to any music as I'd need to keep listening for people closing in behind me on the trail and I knew I would get frustrated standing aside every two minutes to let them past. I could not have picked a worse day to be hiking this section of trail.

I sat watching competitors pass by for half an hour, while I plotted my moves for the day. Looking at the map, I planned a route that took me inland for a few miles, but kept me parallel with the coast path, and it actually turned out to be quite a nice walk over farmland and through tiny hamlets. It wasn't to last too long though, as the inland paths eventually turned north away from the coast and I was forced to head back towards the main trail.

Not ready to be barged along a footpath by sweaty, breathless runners, I took one last chance at a vague, unused trail. The farmland flattened out and I was suddenly surrounded by large, yellow cornfields, one of my favourite places to walk and I smiled, content that I'd made the right choice to pick this path. In my relaxed frame of mind, I must have taken a wrong turn at some point though, as I came across a locked iron gate. There were no obvious signs of any trails the other side of it, just rows of hawthorn bushes and a few rusted vehicles, sitting neglected in an overgrown copse. I was unsure what to do, go back and re-trace my steps, or climb the gate and see where it takes me. Forgetting about my terrible decisions in private Devonshire woodlands some days back, I chose to hop over the gate to have a look. There was no particular direction to walk in, so I followed the path of least resistance, walking on the shortest grass, which took me past some old farming equipment to a high, thorny hedgerow. Realising there was no way I could find my way back to the trail in this direction, I admitted defeat and turned to walk back to the iron gate. As I walked past the farming equipment once again, my heart skipped a beat. I hadn't taken much notice of what it was before, but as I took a long, confused look at each appliance in the field, I saw they were all wired up to a series of car batteries, and each one had a little light, clearly illuminated and blinking at me in the afternoon sun. These were not items of farming equipment after all, they were bird scaring devices, primed and ready to go off at any moment. Living in the countryside, I knew how powerful and loud these things could be, and to be so close to one, would surely have damaged my hearing at the very least, if not hospitalised me. I was so far from any trail that to be injured here would have been a nightmare, I may not have been found for days. I ran like the wind to the iron gate, my pack suddenly not feeling quite as heavy with my life being at risk. After walking swiftly in the direction of the coast, I eventually hit the main path again and breathed a sigh of relief. I never did hear the scarers go off, but the threat was very real....and very scary.

It was getting late in the afternoon and the last dregs of competitors were passing me, tired and probably wondering why they'd even attempted such a gruelling event in such heat. I was even walking as quick as they were running, up some of the steepest coastal sections. The concern for me now was not the runners, but where I was going to set up my tent. I'd been set back a good ten miles and with people still flooding the coast path to cheer people on, it would have been difficult to find somewhere I wouldn't be disturbed or seen. Luckily, though I hadn't noticed it on the map before, I remembered reading about a campsite just off the coast path at Treen and I thought I'd check it out. I wasn't holding my breath though, it was getting late and there were many people around, and so I expected to be turned away with the site being full.

Fortunately, my luck had finally changed. There was one space left on the site in the most perfect spot. Sheltered by high hedges, it was not only wind-free, but it had privacy, and it was close to toilets and the shop, from which I bought food and a bottle of red wine to see me through what might have been a boisterous night. It was not, I'm pleased to say.

After timing my hike so poorly along this section of trail due to the race, I timed my arrival at the campsite perfectly, watching three bedraggled backpackers get turned away literally minutes after I had been shown to my pitch. I felt bad for them, but not guilty. I knew how it felt to be refused a camp pitch, but I think time was on their side to find a suitable spot on the coast somewhere and get a free night, with a beautiful sunset....which I couldn't see due to the high hedges!

SEPTEMBER 6TH

I'd planned to set off early the next morning, having missed a few miles on trail the day before, but on waking at 6am, I heard the thumping of heavy rain upon my tent. It was relentless until at least 9am, the time when I was supposed to be departing from the campsite. I'd gone to the toilet around 7am, to rid my bladder of the bottle of wine, and returned to the tent absolutely saturated. I wondered what had happened to the weather forecast that had given me so much hope for the upcoming days. Do they ever get it right?

Annoyed but determined to get a start on the day, I packed away my tent in driving rain. As gutted as I was to miss out on the sunset the previous evening because of the high hedges, I was now thanking them for giving me some protection from the deluge. I was still wet though, and I thought of the hikers that were refused from the site and who probably had to camp without any protection from the elements. This made me feel a little happier, knowing they may be wetter than me.

Annoyingly, the rain passed over within minutes of me exiting the campsite and the sun glinted in the deep puddles of muddy water on the trail. Maybe I should have waited a little longer in my tent, but it was going to be a soggy start to the day, regardless, until the warmth had dried everything out. I hoped that wouldn't take too long.

It was the passing of Land's End today, the turning of the corner and what would probably make me feel like I was nearing the finish. Of course, Minehead was still many miles away, but the thought of counting *down* the miles, rather than clocking how many I'd already walked, was a completely different prospect and I felt sure it would give me an extra boost of confidence, spurring me on to reach the end.

What spurred me on to pass Land's End more, was the amount of people in the area. It was a beautiful, sunny day and the cliff tops were dotted with hordes of hikers, some quite obviously walking a long distance, others with dogs and small children, clearly there to view the landmark and carrying nothing more than an anorak and a litre of water. I could see why so many people would want to be there in the warm sunshine, the landscape was stunning. Quite barren and rocky, almost apocalyptic in nature, but with a unique beauty and a complete sense of freedom, for me at any rate. That was all to change as I climbed out of a cove and over the headland to view what can only be described as a 'theme park'!

I'd only been to Land's End once as a child, apparently, but I couldn't remember anything about it, and to be honest, I'd have rather it stayed that way. The only moment of interest for me was a model village outside the complex, beautifully crafted to immaculate detail, it was truly outstanding. I've always enjoyed the idea of model making but never took the opportunity to give it a go, due to the fact I'd probably lose my patience after one building. Hats off to those people that spend countless hours, perfecting every little detail of these magnificent miniature wonderlands, and delivering pleasure for many people.

I didn't hang around for too long at Land's End, for obvious reasons, and heading off up the over-crowded coast, I thought it would only be a matter of time before the trail thinned of people and I'd be alone once again. How wrong could I be?

Only a short amount of time passed before I reached the 'even more over-crowded' Sennen Cove. I could barely see the golden grains of the beach along Whitesand Bay, for the amount of people that were sat upon it. Not just the beach itself, but the cramped streets in the village too, teeming with sun worshippers, dressed in shorts and bikini's, trying desperately to brown as much skin on their bodies as possible, although most of them looked quite red to me.

I shuffled through Sennen Cove as quickly as I could and began to climb around Escalls Cliff, which would have been quite a lovely part of trail to walk if it hadn't have been for an elderly lady and, I presumed, her son in front of me. There was a gentle breeze blowing into our faces and it was strong enough to have impaired anybody's hearing of footsteps behind them, but no matter how much noise I made, including a vocal request to pass at certain sections, the lady couldn't hear me....and she was walking frustratingly slow. It

161

was actually quite impressive to see someone of her age and frailty, clambering over the rocky trail, with no assistance from her son at any point. He didn't seem to have any interest in her welfare and walked about twenty yards in front, looking increasingly annoyed every time he turned to see her falling ever further behind. I was preparing myself to aid her if she suffered a stumble or fall, because I'm pretty sure he'd have just rolled his eyes and waved her to get up.

We finally reached a wider section of path and the lady stopped to take a short rest to catch her breath. On doing so, she glanced behind and saw me. I could tell in her eyes that she was sorry to have held me up for so long, but I couldn't blame her at all. She was very friendly and we exchanged a few words of encouragement, while her son looked on with a frown. Now *this* was the moment that made me truly angry...Her son had seen me walking so close behind his mother for some time, knowing that I would be wanting to pass, but never once did he inform her of my presence. Then, after saying my goodbyes to her, I expected him to also let me pass, but he turned back to the trail and completely blocked my way, walking as slow as the lady had been and refusing to budge. Outraged, I was literally two feet behind him for nearly a minute until the trail widened and he looked back for the lady, his eyes completely bypassing mine as if I wasn't even there. Well he certainly knew I was there soon after, as I forced my way by, disgusted with his lack of consideration. I didn't even give him an opportunity to respond as I huffed my way as quickly as I could along the trail. How did such a lovely lady spawn someone so arrogant?!

It's strange how things can change so quickly. The day had begun with a drenching at the campsite, followed by a crowded tourist attraction and an even more crowded tourist village. My irritation levels were high after that, but were charged even further by being held up by an inconsiderate idiot, and so I didn't expect the day to get any better. I couldn't have been more wrong. The trail opened out to stunning rocky landscapes, fewer people and a return to a happier mood than I'd had since before Falmouth. It was one of my favourite afternoons on trail and I was relishing everything it had to offer.

I walked through an area of disused mine shafts and quarries and the industrial landscape around me made my heart pound with excitement. The sun was lowering in the sky and all around me, the eerie shadows from brick chimneys and abandoned buildings stretched across the land. I decided it was time for a bit of music, and I could think of no better album to listen to than Depeche Mode's 'Construction Time Again', a favourite of mine and one that evoked a sense of empathy with the miners that used to work in this tough environment. Before I knew it, the album had finished and I found myself hitting the replay button, it felt that powerful.

The entire section between Cape Cornwall and Pendeen Watch is something that will stay with me forever. I don't know whether the time of day would make any difference if I decided to revisit, but that late afternoon sun, glaring so bright over the cliff tops was perfect.

I found a perfect camp spot on a tiny area of grass, amidst the prickly gorse above Tregaminion Cliff. Apart from the copious amounts of sheep droppings I had to swipe away with my shoe, the pitch was incredible, although fairly close to the path, but it was on a remote section and I didn't think anyone would be passing so late and I certainly didn't see or hear anyone. It would've taken an explosion to take my eyes off the stunning sunset over the calm sea that night, anyway.

SEPTEMBER 7TH

Getting lost on trail is always frustrating, but when it happens within the first few steps on a brand new day, it's downright annoying. Having a plan in my head to walk a certain amount of miles, to get to a certain area that looks good to camp, is something I spend a while doing after pitching my tent and having food every evening. It's an essential part of the journey, knowing where the trail will take you, what food supply options there are and if there are fresh water sources on the way. I'd followed the same routine the previous night, so to be standing in the middle of a cattle field at 6.30am, wondering where i'd gone wrong just minutes after setting off, is beyond my comprehension. There were no signposts, no obvious markers and even though I had a map in front of me, I couldn't for the life of me work out where I was in relation to it all. The only point of reference I had was the sea and where the dank landscape bumped into it, and so, as I had seemingly walked slightly inland for some reason, I chose to make a bee line for the coast and hope that I'd find my way. Thankfully, after saturating my feet in long grass covered in morning dew, clambering over a padlocked gate and dodging countless cow pats, I found the coast path once again. It still baffles me how I lost the original trail so easily, and I put it down to morning fog, not in a weather sense, but in my head. I'd had these kinds of mornings before, where something may not have been quite right, but I plodded on regardless and paid in consequence thereafter. With it not being a new phenomenon, I scanned the path behind me and the direction I'd walked to get to that point, shrugged my shoulders with an acceptance of defeat in the matter, and continued on my way without any more thought to my incompetence.

My intended camping spot the day before had been Black Head. It looked relatively flat on the map and quite suitable, although my legs would have struggled to get me there, and I am eternally grateful for my aching limbs to have gotten the better of me. On arrival, even though the mist and chilly winds had taken the edge off the bounty that I had been expecting, it was with great relief that I concluded it would have been a terrible idea. Flat?...yes. Perfect?...by no means. Not only was there very few places to pitch a tent without worrying about rips from the sharp gorse bushes, but the field was full to the brim of cows, something I would have had to endure on my awakening in the morning. They were everywhere, and I could only imagine what the sound of many hooved creatures around my tent at 5am would have been like. Unnerving for a start.

I'd had a bit of a cow phobia in the past after being chased across fields by them on many occasions. It was down to a video I watched before setting off on my journey, that the fear had been eased slightly, and putting into practise some of the tips I'd seen, had worked so far on the trail: Don't make too much noise and just keep walking; Never run; If they still trot towards you, then shouting aggressively and moving towards *them* would stop them in their tracks. I'd also been told that all they really want to do is play, but the jury is still out on that one, and to be honest, I can't seem them being interested in chasing a tennis ball or a large stick!

I moved slowly through the herd on Black Head, stepping aside for some of the largest beasts on the headland and worrying that the inquisitive calves, who edged ever nearer to me out of curiosity, would attract the attention of their mothers and possibly cause her to be aggressive towards me, even though I wasn't provoking the youngsters of course. I'm not sure she would understand the concept of blame though and they're quite obviously too large to quibble with. After hopping swiftly over a creaky stile, I was back out into open country and back on the right path.

The trail to Zennor Head was some of the hardest I'd dealt with up to that point, made more difficult by the stiffening cold breeze, and constant drizzle all morning. I was soaked through to the bone and had that raw feeling of chill, that seemed to invade every bone in my body and made me question if I'd ever feel warm again. For five miles, the weather was relentless and I rarely found any shelter for respite. As a sufferer of Raynaud's Disease, which can affect the fingers to the point where they turn white and painfully numb, it was agony. No amount of blowing on my hands with warm breath, or trying to shake my arms to get the blood circulating properly, would ease the symptoms, and it was getting so bad that I was beginning to feel a little sick. At one point I decided I could take no more and I needed to address the situation as a matter of urgency. My answer was a hot cup of coffee in the hope that it would warm me up inside, and that I could also ease the pain in my fingers by holding the hot plastic cup. Opening my pack to get out the stove was a little tricky with a limited amount of digit movement. Being wet and cold, I could barely squeeze my fingers together to unclasp the strap buckles, and as for firing up my lighter....

I finally managed a seat on the driest rock I could find and enjoyed the best cup of coffee I'd tasted in some time. I could feel every sip thawing out my insides and the beginnings of blood circulating freely again around my hands, as my fingers began to tingle. I knew what was coming though, and I prepared myself accordingly, by swinging my arms in wide circles around me. This was going to be painful, as the ghostly colour of my fingers turned back to a deep red, and the tingling sensation would turn to a throbbing. I'd been here before and although it's a very painful few minutes, there is actually a sense of relief too, knowing that I'd have feelings in my extremities once again. Putting things back into my pack was certainly a lot easier, that's for sure.

Unfortunately, the trail didn't get any easier. Quite often, it felt like I was back in my beloved Peak District, the path being very similar to that of the Pennine Way, rocky and lined with heather, and indeed, the murky conditions. In many ways I felt comforted by this, despite its unforgiving nature. With mist rolling in constantly over the cliff tops, hindering my view of the trail ahead, every now and again it would briefly part to give me a panoramic treasure, which warmed my heart more than any coffee could. The solitude and the spectacular scenery was one of the reasons I chose this trail and once again my spirits were lifted. After a thorough drenching throughout the morning, the magnificence of what this trail holds was shining through. I'd like to say that that continued for the rest of the day, but of course, it did not.

I was just a few miles from St. Ives when the sun finally broke through the gloom, and it almost seemed that the entire town itself was waiting for that one event. Now I'm sure you've heard the rhyme and riddle 'As i was going to St. Ives'? It could not have been more appropriate. I came across so many people walking the path in the opposite direction, and having to step aside to let them pass was getting downright annoying. When you're the only one going to St. Ives, and you're meeting a man and seven women and twenty dogs and fifty kids (or however the rhyme goes), it always has to be the solitary person that yields, and I was most definitely the *only* person heading to the town. At one point I decided to count the amount of people I met, and in a period of around ten minutes, I lost count at around fifty.

I didn't like St. Ives particularly, it's cramped, over-crowded and felt quite hostile, possibly due to the amount of tourists, but I was quite relieved to escape the trail and walk through the town, finding a back street pub and stopping for some food. It had been a difficult morning at times, beautiful at others, but the sheer amount of people on trail in the late morning had been the major factor for me and I couldn't wait to get back to the solitude I'd so often craved on the journey.

The weather had improved considerably by the time I left the pub. The wind had died down and the sun was very hot, a world away from the cold and drizzle I experienced earlier in the day. My clothing and gear soon dried and I even changed into my shorts for the remainder of the day, stealthfully changing in a sand dune away from the prying eyes of sun-worshippers that crowded the afternoon beaches. What I failed to see in my haste to find some privacy, was a golf course, and a large group of men in high spirits, that were now applauding each others' putting on the green that overlooked the dune I sat in. Clearly, they had been out of sight on the fairway at the time I'd chosen my spot, but it now felt like they were clapping me, as I slipped my shorts on, red-faced. Even though I was sure the applause was not for me, I nearly took a bow in honour of their appreciation, but decided against drawing any more attention to myself.

A long road walk around Hayle Estuary awaited me, before the trail headed back towards the sea and into yet more sand dunes. I wasn't too keen to be walking on sand for any amount of time after an exhausting morning around Zennor Head, and so I swiftly decided to keep to the main road, which would mean I could walk faster, even if it wasn't quite as direct as the trail itself. Having never walked the coastal path on this section, I was unsure if I had chosen wisely or not, but nevertheless, I plodded on amidst the roar of rush hour traffic, averting my eyes to the stares of rough-looking locals as they filed out of the run down convenience stores with their bags full of cheap ale. I didn't feel very safe at all here and it had taken me by surprise. Even though St. Ives had felt a little unfriendly, it had been a cordial experience compared to Hayle, and I was now wishing that I'd stuck to the coast path and endured the sand beneath my feet.

At the first opportunity, I took a footpath that headed back to the sea and I was greeted with the most incredible sunset across the water. The golden sun shimmered brightly on the crest of each rolling wave and flashes of orange and ochre within each ripple of the blackened tide filled me with awe. It was the perfect ending to a rather stressful day, and not even the worry of finding somewhere to camp that night could take away the gift nature had provided me. These were the moments I cherished, and they made even the toughest days bearable. I was thankful to be treated by the shining panoramic views until the last glint of the suns corona disappeared beyond the horizon, leaving me content and appreciative of all that this beautiful coastline had to offer.

SEPTEMBER 8TH

Before the first rays of sun had blessed the morning skies on this new day, I had already walked a couple of miles. I was intending on getting as close to Newquay as I could, but without entering the town itself. I'd seen a couple of campsites on the map, just slightly inland and off the trail and so I was aiming for one of those, in the hope they could squeeze me in for the coming night.

I arrived in Portreath early and was very thankful to see a line of public toilets along the main road. Opting to set off before the dawn had meant I'd declined any bathroom opportunities amidst the gorse bushes, and I was glad I did, as it was nice to be able to seat myself on clean plastic, rather than straddle awkwardly over a six inch hole in spiky, wet grass. As I entered a toilet (chosen at random) I noticed the row of houses across the street, all facing in my direction, and I suddenly felt a wave of paranoia hit me, as though every resident was peering from behind their curtain, watching me and chanting 'We know what you're doing!' As I sat to do my business, I then had visions of them taking out their stopwatches and timing me. Very unnatural thoughts for a very natural function, I concluded, but still I rushed to finish, and departed steathfully with an embarrassed grimace, even though I doubted any curtain had been twitched and no timing equipment had been used.

I really enjoyed the following few miles on trail. The weather was beautiful and I had seen barely a soul since Portreath. Finding a fast flowing steam, that headed briskly towards the sea over solid rock, was a bonus. With a few pieces of grubby clothing in my bag, I thought it was a good time to have a short break and do some laundry. It wouldn't be long until I reached Newquay and was able to get to a launderette to do it properly, but knowing I'd have at least one more night under the stars, which may also be in a campsite with many other people, and the fact I had to travel through Perranporth (which I knew to be a popular tourist destination), I wanted to at least try and be wearing something that didn't smell like a cats crotch.

With shirts and socks dangling from my pack, I arrived at St. Agnes Head. The sun had gotten considerably hotter and the hills considerably steeper. The number of people cramming the trails along the cliff edges was overwhelming at times, but I could appreciate why they came here, especially in wonderful weather, the scenery was incredible. In fact, all the way from St. Agnes Head to Cligga Head was stunning. Just like Cape Cornwall, it was an area that had been used for mining and the old buildings still stood majestically, dominating the rugged landscape.

The moment I had been dreading all day was upon me, Perran Beach. It's amazing that everyone I had told previously about my upcoming adventure, seemed to ask if I was going to Perranporth. My reply was simply, "If it's on the coast, then the chances are I'll be going there", and that seemed to make them excited. Why? I have no idea, it was hell on earth for me. I could barely see the sand at the southernmost section for the amount of sun worshippers, and I had the daunting task of plotting a route through the middle of them all. There was no way around. Over beach towels, around sand castles and deck chairs, I threaded my way through the chaos, making every effort to not step on bare toes and fingers with each step. The stationary beach dwellers were one challenge, but when I had several people head straight towards me carrying beers and surf boards, that made things even more difficult. The sand was so soft and uneven due to the amount of foot traffic, that it seemed to take twice as much energy to lift my feet, and with every stride, I was taking on more and more sand into my shoes. For a good fifteen minutes I was really struggling with the whole situation. At times I felt like screaming, although I probably wouldn't have been heard due to the amount of children doing the same, although theirs would have been with enjoyment and mine in complete agony.

The crowds finally thinned as I neared Perran Sands Holiday Centre, but the sandy nightmare would continue for another two miles, for this was one of Cornwall's longest beaches and there was no other route I could take to spare me from the torture. It was relentless and very exhausting. I kept looking back to

Perranporth itself and it never looked like getting any further away. Finally, the arduous flat trek gave way to dunes and a steep climb onto the Ligger Point peninsular. I was so tired but very relieved. The hoards of people were now just a dot on the shimmering horizon and I was alone once again to enjoy the late afternoon splendour across the sea, and the peace and quiet.

On the cliff tops stood Penhale Camp. It was an eerie, derelict place, surrounded by a two metre high fence and previously used for military personnel, right back to the Second World War. I walked with widened eyes, fixed on the crumbling buildings, in awe of events that must have occurred here. I have since learned that 23 soldiers were killed in a bombing raid by the German Luftwaffe in 1940 on that very spot.

It was due to the over-whelming nature of the camp and my constant intrigue, that it was only at the very last second I noticed something squirming around on the trail in front of me. Startled, I came to a halt. It was a snake of some kind, and it looked in distress, maybe due to a pair of large shoes heading straight for it! Not being confident in identifying the creature, I presumed it to be a smooth snake and I was unsure as to it's nature. I therefore didn't want to get too close to it, but I really wanted to help. It wouldn't have been long before a circling gull would have picked it off and so I tried desperately to remove it from the trail using just my trekking pole. This was a fruitless venture to say the least. It was like picking up a worm with a toothpick. I tried to flick it into the grass, wait until it had wrapped itself around the pole and lift it to safety, and even tried to nudge it to encourage its direction, all without success. There was no way I was going to pick it up with my hands and I didn't fancy a set of fangs gnawing on my toes through my soft shoes by trying to sweep it off the path, and so I had to leave it to fend for itself. After some research, I realised it was actually a slow worm and of no threat to me at all. I could have probably scooped it up in my hands and been perfectly safe. I hope it survived.

It wasn't long before I arrived in the tiny beachside hamlet of Holywell.

It was an idyllic setting with high sand dunes and lapping waves in a quaint cove. It was at this point that I headed inland to find my chosen campsite for the coming evening. It wasn't ideal, considering I'd recently trudged three miles along Perran Beach, but I chose a trail that headed through the sand dunes, as this seemed the most direct route according to the map. After only a few minutes, it became apparent that my map, gps on my phone *and* the trail signs were not in agreement with each other. Stubbornly I pressed on along the only clear trail I could see, following a lady walking her dog. I figured she must be local and assumed she'd be able to lead me to the other side of the dunes. Suddenly, she stopped and turned around. The dog gave me a curious look with a confused head tilt and without any further interaction, she walked past me and returned in the direction she'd already come. I was now on my own to work out which map source was telling the truth. I thought it may be a little odd if I was to turn around and follow the lady back, and so I continued along a trail which got narrower and less defined...very quickly.

I'm happy to say that the trail eventually opened out to fields and a definite path towards a golf course. I continued on, still a little unsure of my direction but feeling more confident now I could see where I was heading. I'm not sure how I managed it to this day, but I ended up in Tevornick Caravan Park, completely the wrong direction I was hoping for. Seeing a few tents dotted around the site, I considered enquiring about a pitch, but I had the feeling it would have been a very expensive night, and possibly not an enjoyable one either. I came across a water tap, filled a litre and decided to push on to my desired camp site, albeit an extra couple of miles due to my disorientation.

After crossing fields (and unintentionally following another lady with a dog) I finally arrived at a narrow, leafy road. Through the bows of large oak trees I saw civilization. Well, rented chalets and caravans. It was a campsite, and it looked very nice. Although it wasn't the site I had pinpointed for a stay, it looked good enough to me, and I definitely chose wisely.

I walked towards the main reception, but before I could get there, a gentleman on a small waist-height tractor had spotted me and was making his way swiftly to my location. I waited for him to arrive, as it was obvious he was the site owner. I asked if there was any availability and I was greeted with the soothing words "Of course".

As I followed him into the reception to make my payment, he asked if I was hiking the coast path and that he would only charge me five pounds if that was the case. I ended up paying eight though as he couldn't do the five deal if I was paying by card. Still, eight pounds for a great campsite like this was fantastic. While processing the transaction he informed me it was pizza night at the site shop. I was ecstatic. Not only a shop where I could resupply for the following day, but I could also buy beer and eat a home-cooked pizza. It was a pleasant nights stay, I can tell you that!

SEPTEMBER 9TH

I was expecting to wake early the following morning due to being on a campsite, and although the weather was fine and I was surrounded on three sides by holidaymakers, my eyes opened around 8am. Maybe it was the bottle of wine, the large pizza and the exhaustion of Perran Beach the day before that took it's toll on my sleep pattern.

I'd packed everything away by 9am and hit a side trail towards the village of Crantock. There was an easy route back to the coast path, but it meant more hiking over sand dunes, and just the mere thought of that filled me with dread, and so I accepted the fact I'd be walking along some roads for a while, with the knowledge it would be flat and would ease me into my seven mile hike into Newquay. Things would have been a little more pleasant if I'd have paid closer attention the sign posts in the centre of Crantock, as I took the wrong fork and headed along the busy Halwyn Road and not the intended route towards Penpol. I couldn't understand why the traffic had increased so much, to the point where I was standing to one side to let cars pass at regular intervals, until I realised my mistake. By then it was too late, it was quicker to carry on along the main road than to retrace my steps. The road narrowed in places and was becoming more dangerous. Traffic was having to stop because I had nowhere to step off the tarmac. It was getting very frustrating and I endured the stress for at least an hour before I was able to take a side road, which thankfully led me directly to the coast path, where I could continue my journey along a more peaceful bridleway.

The quiet wasn't to last long as I crossed a footbridge over the estuary and immediately hit the main road into Newquay. It was on a slight uphill gradient and the solid ground beneath my feet was arduous. I'd only walked six miles but already I was feeling aches in my calves and thighs.

Thankfully, salvation was close. I had booked myself into the cheapest bed and breakfast I could find, Berties Lodge. It was a strange place to say the least and was accessed through an adjourning hotel lobby, which took me quite a while to work out, but I eventually approached the reception desk to make my enquiries. As I joined a small queue of customers, I suddenly became aware of an angry lady at the head of the line, who was clearly unhappy about her situation, and was directing a torrent of abuse toward the timid girl behind the desk. Her situation was no secret as her raging tones echoed around the lobby and I glanced at other people with raised eyebrows. It was soon apparent that the hotel had split her four-person family into separate rooms and she demanded they find her a new, single room for them all, which she claimed had been booked for a number of months. Her fury was so intense that her eyes had welled with tears and I began

181

to find some sympathy for her. I have no idea how it eventually turned out, but after making a couple of phone calls, the receptionists solution had calmed the lady down somewhat. As she stepped aside and wiped her eyes, waiting for the hotel manager I presumed, I shuffled to the desk, dragging my pack across the polished tiles. The receptionists' hands were shaking slightly but her face seemed very relieved as I simply enquired about my check-in time. I was a little concerned that my booking would not be on their system after hearing the bitterness from the sobbing lady, but all was well.

Having a couple of hours to kill, I decided to head directly across the road to the launderette, unload all my grubby clothes into a washing machine and then make a bee line for the Griffin Inn, just a short hop away. I'd got time for one swift pint before my clothes were washed, then I returned to place them into a dryer, before heading back to the pub for a meal and another pint. It was all timed to perfection. When the check-in time approached, I had a full stomach and a full set of clean clothes.

I collected my room key from the reception desk and headed up a flight of stairs, which led to a long corridor. After going through a couple of sets of swing doors, around several corners, up another small set of stairs, through what looked like a fire door (which was concerning as I wasn't sure I'd be able to get back through it once it had closed behind me), and across a smaller, creaky-floored corridor, I arrived at my number. I'd obviously now entered Berties Lodge through the maze of chambers that connected it to the main hotel. Still a little worried should a fire alarm sound, I opened the stiff, creaking door to my digs, and I wasn't disappointed at all. A shower, a tv, a comfy bed, sockets to charge my batteries and a stunning sea view across Newquay Bay. It was well worth every penny I'd paid.

SEPTEMBER 10TH

After a cup of coffee and a lengthy hot shower, I vacated my room at Berties Lodge and navigated the labyrinth of corridors and stairs, exiting the hotel lobby around 9am into bright, warm sunshine. With the final ferry crossing of my journey firmly fixed in my mind, my mission was to travel at least 23 miles to Padstow, across the estuary and beyond to Polzeath, and so I was grateful to feel fully refreshed and clean, although with no breakfast facilities at the lodge, I was forced to take a number of mid-morning breaks for snacks to keep my energy levels up. No hardship in lovely weather with gorgeous views of course.

It was getting late in the afternoon when I realised I'd been a little too liberal with my steps and underestimated the distance I still had to travel. The beautiful coastline around Trenance, Porthcothan and Trevose Head had seriously dented my chances of reaching the Padstow ferry on time, the last trip of the day being 7pm. I'd taken far too many breaks to admire the scenery and I was now under pressure to reach my goal, needing to cover nearly nine miles in less than four hours. I took a large glug of water, unwrapped an energy bar and focused on the challenge at hand.

It can be a little deflating when you can see your destination in the far distance, but don't seem to be getting there very fast. This was certainly the case as I rounded Stepper Point and I found myself checking the time constantly. With about forty minutes left before the ferry departed, and just over a mile of walking to go, I finally relaxed. I was just going to make it. What I'd failed to take into consideration, was which ferry point to wait at. There was two possible places and I didn't know which one was the 7pm departure point. With time at a premium, I headed for the first terminal along the estuary, near St. Saviour's Point. Gazing across the waters, I couldn't see any signs of movement and started to panic a little. With nobody else waiting on the slipway with me, I came to the conclusion I was at the wrong location, and swiftly made my way further into the town. It proved to be the right decision, and as I approached Padstow harbour walls, I saw the ferry sailing across the bay towards me. It was such a relief, as the sun was beginning to sink on the horizon.

The journey across the estuary was brief but very pleasant in the evening stillness and I alighted at the tiny village of Rock on the opposite bank with about eighty minutes of daylight left. My dilemma now was the three mile walk to my chosen camping spot on Pentire Point, which would take me through a bustling Polzeath. It was clear that I wouldn't make it before dark but plodded on regardless.

With headtorch at the ready, I entered the built up area. The streets were heaving with pub-goers and holiday makers. Thankfully, nobody seemed to be interested in me, although I felt a similar unease to that of my time waiting for the bus in Torquay. I frequently had to check the map on my phone to make sure I was still on the coast path as I was directed through sinister, narrow streets and threatening alleyways, and every time I did this, a bright glow from the screen lit up my face and affected my night vision. It took several seconds before I could see clearly enough to move on in the darkened passageways and I felt a little vulnerable at times.

I'm pleased to say I reached the small beach cove of Pentireglaze Haven, just as the last light of day clung to the evening skies. There was a large group of young people on the beach, drinking and dancing to loud music beside a roaring log fire that lit the cliffs ahead with an orange hue. I was wary about passing them to begin with, but they were enjoying themselves too much to care about me. I was actually pleased they were there, as the glow from the fire assisted my journey on the incline to Pentire Point. As the firelight faded, I didn't know if I was being watched while ascending into the blackness, with the beam from my headtorch being the only indication I was there on the cliffside, and now making me visible for miles around. I certainly didn't intend to make the trek without it though, as the path rose higher from the cove below.

I reached the pinnacle after about twenty minutes. As I climbed, the sky seemed to brighten once again now I had a view of the horizon, but it didn't last long, soon my only comfort was my torchlight and the gentle shimmer from the lights in the town behind me. The beach fire was a mere dot of light, that flickered as people danced around it and intermittently blocked it from my view. I didn't spend too long admiring the scenery though. The wind had picked up slightly and I needed to pitch my tent as soon as possible. I had no idea what the lay of the land was or if there were any cattle in the fields, I had to do it all in near darkness, but apart from a few thistles and spiky bramble underfoot, I was happy with my location.

After checking my map and pedometer, I realised I'd walked over 28 miles. At times like that, it was usually necessary to have a meal, but I was quite exhausted and just felt like sleeping. I forced a bag of Pistachio nuts down me. At least I was going to get a shot of protein and crucial fats to assist my body the following morning. As I sat crunching away, building up a huge pile of empty shells at my tent door, I gazed upon the glittering town at the foot of the cove. I'd experienced a stark emotional contrast within the last hour, I thought, and that it takes solitude upon a cliff top to make me feel completely safe. I just hoped the field I sat in was cow-free!

SEPTEMBER 11TH

I unzipped my tent at first light, unaware of what may lay outside due to pitching in the dark the previous evening. I was pleased to see that I'd camped sufficiently far enough from the coast path that I wouldn't have been disturbed by dog walkers or runners, and even more pleased to see the field was devoid of large beasts that may have had me panicking in the early hours. Despite the lack of luminance while choosing my spot, it was clear I'd picked the best location I could have hoped for. It was time for a cup of coffee and some breakfast in the knowledge I'd be fine for another hour or so at least.

Clambering over the mound of Pistachio shells in the tent doorway, I was ready to break camp around 7am. Still no sign of any other life in the vicinity, I eased my aching limbs, one at a time, onto the soft grass outside and rolled the rest of me through the doorway in a very ungracious manner, almost pulling the tent on top of me as I caught the flysheet under my right hip.

I stretched my legs, back, arms and shoulders, yawned until I felt the muscles in my face sting and then sat beside my tent, looking out across the ocean to a beautiful morning. After walking so far the day before and not having too many hours sleep, I felt very lethargic, but I had two places of interest on the agenda, the village of Port Isaac and the legendary

Tintagel. I had been looking forward to seeing these places since I first set off from Poole, and that was the only motivation I needed for the day.

The motivation increased with every footstep as I neared Port Quin. It was one of the most scenic parts of the trail I'd encountered since Dorset. The trail itself was a well-defined, six inch ribbon of grit that snaked its way across the lush green hills, and I was in awe. I could have happily sat and gazed at the path in front of me all day. These were the times that I realised why I hiked trails, the feeling it gave me was a homely one, a sense of belonging and a burning desire to find out what was beyond. I was an explorer, stepping upon undiscovered lands. My heart was thumping with excitement.

The trail did not disappoint for the following few miles and as I rounded Lobber Point on the approach to Port Isaac, I came across a bench overlooking the harbour. It was the perfect place to take an extended break and enjoy the views to the village and the surrounding hills that it nestled in.

One of the reasons I had been looking forward to seeing Port Isaac, is the fact it is the filming location for the popular drama Doc Martin. I had only recently began to watch the programme with interest, but after viewing one, I was instantly hooked. It wasn't until I'd planned the coast path walk and did some research, that I learned about the filming locations of such tv shows and so it was quite a thrill to know I would be passing through this little gem of a village, and who knew, maybe they would even be filming when I arrived?!

I'd been sat on the bench for nearly an hour, intensely watching the harbour and the many people milling around, trying to ascertain if camera's were in use. I was just too far away to determine what people were doing, despite a couple of them waving arms around in a directorial manner. The only way I was going to find out for sure, is to get off my butt and walk into the village.

One of the first houses I passed, was the home of Doc Martin himself. A grey stone building with red brick edging around the windows and doors. I remember admiring the building, although I continued past without stopping, not realising it's significance in the show. As I approached the harbour, it was teeming with tourists. I was suddenly overwhelmed. From the bench high on the hillside, the village looked quite placid, but now I was right in the mix, and even though it was still relatively early in the day, I struggled to weave through the narrow streets with my hefty pack.

I was quite hungry at this point and decided to take my chances in a pasty shop, hoping there'd be more space inside than out on the bustling pavement. Thankfully, this was the case and I was instantly welcomed by a young lady behind the counter. I pondered my choices for a few seconds, viewing a board packed with food options, but I think I knew what I wanted before I'd even stepped through the doorway. I had been in Cornwall for quite a while now, yet I'd never sampled a proper pasty. It was time. With hot pastry in a thin paper bag burning my fingers, I exited the shop to find some space to devour my breakfast. The pasty would be warm for quite some time, and so I headed out of the village along cobbled streets to find some solitude. As I climbed towards the cliff tops and Port Gaverne, the traffic increased tenfold. I had made the right choice.

It's not difficult to understand the attraction that people have to their favourite tv show filming locations. Even though the shows are generally fictional, people need that tangibility. A brief glimpse, or even the ability to touch something they've seen on television can make them feel connected, and suddenly the fiction becomes a reality in their minds. The local shop owners passionately tap into this of course, offering all kinds of gifts displaying photo's of lead characters and properties with the 'as seen on tv' theme. Mugs, keyrings, postcards and pictures, all providing a permanent reminder of a visit to Port Isaac. For me, it was a juicy Cornish Pasty that filled my stomach to the brim and fuelled me for the coming hours along the coast path, and even though it didn't have Martin Clunes' face on it, it was all I needed from the picturesque fishing village.

I wasn't really prepared for the exertion to come within the following few miles. It was a beautiful area, but it was a rollercoaster. Every crest I reached meant another descent into a valley, and a total ascent of well over 2000ft lay spread across the hills ahead of me. Even a lengthy drinks break at Trebarwith Strand could not refresh me in the soaring afternoon heat. I thought back to the day before and how many miles I had covered to get past Padstow, and how little sleep I'd had on Pentire Point. It was then I realised just how exhausted I'd become, but I was so close to Tintagel now, I felt I must push on. I'm pleased I did, there were very limited options for camping around Trebarwith and with Tintagel being a popular destination for tourists, I'd have been setting up my tent in the dark again after waiting for everyone to go home, and tonight, I really needed a good nights sleep.

I arrived in Tintagel late afternoon with surprisingly few people around. I could see the incredible bridge spanning the gorge between the mainland and the jagged headland, linking modern day with the legendary associations of King Arthur. It was all quite breathtaking, being aware that this area was such a prominent historical site and I couldn't wait to get closer. Unfortunately, I had arrived a little too late in the day to access the bridge across to the settlement remains and I was gutted to say the least. However, as I stood at the locked entrance above the deep ravine and the crashing waves below, I could still gauge a sense of affinity with the surroundings and the people that once inhabited the area. I closed my eyes and let my other senses soak it all in; the wind whistling in my ears, the smell of the salt from the angry sea and the feel of ancient igneous rock on the palms of my hands provided a brief empathy for those earlier civilisations. I could have stayed there for quite a while, absorbing the atmosphere and the relaxing ambience, if it wasn't for a couple of pre-teen girls, who decided to stand right next to me and squeal their lungs out across the chasm, hoping for an echo I presumed. I looked at them with an aversion that I'm not sure they understood, annoyed that they had destroyed a moment of reflection and appreciation for my surroundings. Even my angry wrinkled nose did nothing to prevent further yells across the gorge and I turned, defeated, and headed back to the trail.

SEPTEMBER 12TH

After a very windy night upon Firebeacon Hill, I was quite excited by my next port of call, Boscastle. It was another place I'd pinpointed to take a small diversion to and check out. On 16th August 2004, the sleepy village was subjected to horrific flash-flooding after biblical amounts of rain fell in a short period and caused major damage to properties within the valley, as well as surrounding areas, Rocky Valley and Crackington Haven. The tragic event was captured by film makers and was heavily reported on national news, so to see the village with my own eyes was going to be a moving experience.

I guess a lot had changed in sixteen years, and as I descended to the village along sloping hillsides, the only thing I really recognised from the television coverage was the main harbour and the way the road meandered through the grey stone buildings, although that was obviously the path of least resistance for the huge amounts of flood water, and had now been replaced in my memory by tarmac since I last laid eyes on the hamlet. It was still an eerie feeling as I set foot on the pavements and crossed a small stone bridge, before walking solemnly along the main street towards the local store. As I glanced at buildings, still standing and repaired after the floods, I noticed commemorative plaques on their walls, in remembrance of that dreadful day. Many buildings were not as fortunate and had to be demolished, if they hadn't already been destroyed by the floods.

I didn't stay too long that morning, but as I climbed out of the valley, I looked back several times and silently gave my respects to all the villagers that were affected by the disaster. It's incredible how poignant something becomes when you get to see it with your own eyes and it doesn't matter how many years pass, the emotion still runs high. My thoughts were echoed a few miles further along the coast as I passed through the smaller village of Crackington Haven.

A pleasant hike across hill tops with a lovely warm breeze followed for several miles, though my thoughts seemed to be overtaken by what lay ahead further up the coast. I had read text and viewed many videos on what had been called 'the toughest section' of the coast path. It sounded daunting and it was one of the reasons I opted to hike the trail in this direction, so that my legs would be accustomed to the steepness and, hopefully, I would enjoy it more and not stress as much about getting injuries.

Before I even arrived at Bude, a small sign, which I nearly missed, told me of a path closure. It was not what I needed after walking nearly fifteen miles already, especially as the diversion took me along the coast road, and at least three miles of concrete beneath my feet lay ahead. There were no options. With my head down, I put one foot in front of the other and hoped that music would see me through without any aches or pain, until I reached town for food and water supplies. I had never been so grateful to see a built up area, and especially a small store that I had just managed to catch before they closed for the evening. Stocking up on a few snacks, water and a couple of beers to celebrate my five hundred mile crossing, I remembered I had run out of toilet paper. The only packs the store had came in fours, and I wasn't prepared to carry four whole loo rolls when I only needed one. I purchased the entire pack, but offered three of the rolls to the owners of the shop, for their own personal use. I'm not sure they quite understood why I needed to do that, despite it being clearly obvious I was a hiker, but I squeezed the single roll into my pack and said my goodbyes.

I supped one of my beers on Meer Down as I gazed upon the setting sun over the ocean. I still had over an hour til dusk and only three miles to walk to my chosen camp spot, near a government satellite ground station, which is reported to be involved in all kinds of undercover operations, dealing with MI5 and eavesdropping on civilian communications, to name but a few. I could clearly see the giant white dishes, sitting dominantly upon Harscott High Cliff, so I had a marker to aim for. Although I was quite exhausted and had walked quite a distance throughout the day, it gave me a goal and spurred me on.

It was a lovely evening and the landscape was captivating. Rolling hills to my right and long stretches of beach, hugging the rocky shoreline to my left. I came across a rather strange campsite, that seemed to have no facilities whatsoever. Just copious amounts of tents, campervans and caravans pitched in the middle of an undulating field. Everyone was cooking on throw-away barbeques and having a seemingly wonderful time drinking, as I could tell from the amount of beer cans strewn across the grass beside each pitch. I wondered what these people did when they needed to go to the bathroom. There was absolutely nothing in the way of a toilet, not even a portable one in the corner of the field. I imagined they would have paid at least twenty quid a night for such a spot so close to Bude, but would rue their choice of location once the beers had made their journey 'south'! I must admit, I did chuckle to myself and shake my head in disbelief as I shuffled past. My amusement was to be justified very soon, as I found a lovely spot to camp, literally over the next hill at Warren Gutter, where it was sheltered, quiet and where I was able to enjoy the most incredible sunset....and had no privacy issues when *my* beers went south!

NORTH DEVON
&
SOMERSET

SEPTEMBER 13TH

The next few miles were most definitely some of the hardest on the entire trail. I'd climbed a multitiude of steep hills up to this point, but nothing can prepare you for the intensity of that section. It was a rollercoaster of acclivity. A near-vertical drop into a valley, led almost immediately to a climb of equal gradient on the other side. Thigh-burning wooden steps etched into the hillside were of some comfort to begin with, but after a while, they became a chore, having to lift each leg high and stretch out with every forward motion to reach the next, all while carrying a weighty pack on my back. I think I lost count of the times I uttered the question 'Really?' on that day, bewildered by the topography that lay ahead. There seemed to be no let up. Hill after hill, step after step, droplet of sweat after droplet of sweat. It was a beautiful area, I cannot deny it, and I certainly got plenty of chances to take in the amazing scenery during every break I was forced to take, due to lack of breath and a pounding heart, but man, was it tough!

After a gruelling six miles in intense heat, I finally reached a momentous milestone. It was the Cornwall and Devon border. I realised at that point that I'd walked the entire Cornish coastline without a break, and it had taken me just seventeen days. I was actually quite impressed with my progress, but I have to say, I was more pleased to be back in Devon than of that achievement. In fact, I would go as far as saying, I was relieved to be out of Cornwall.

Cornwall is nice and I understand why people would want to live there, or travel there on a yearly basis for their holiday, but for me, Devon felt more homely and apart from one last steep climb after the border, the trail flattened out across the cliff tops once again, and that was most certainly welcomed. Over Knap Head, around Nabor Point and across Milford Common, I picked up the pace. The trail was effortless and the sun was now tolerable, but I worried about one major lapse in planning, I was running very low on food and water.

I took a break upon St. Catherine's Tor and consulted the map. While doing so, a couple of elderly day hikers passed by and, assuming they were locals, I sought their wisdom regarding local amenities. It wasn't good news. I was quite a distance away from the nearest shop in the village of Hartland, some three miles inland. I looked at the map once more to get my bearings and make a decision, and noticed there was a small campsite in Stoke, which was en route to

Hartland anyway and over two miles nearer. After checking the campsite website on the internet, I read that it had an on-site shop with everything that I would need for my journey. The decision wasn't hard to make. I hadn't wanted to stay on a campsite again on my journey, but with this one being so close to the coast and my supplies running so low, it made sense to head in their direction.

I arrived at the Stoke Barton campsite relatively early in the afternoon and immediately headed straight to the reception to book in. It was a little pricey for what it was and its location, but my mind was made up and this would relieve me of any stress about re-supplying and finding somewhere to wild camp for the night. I happily handed over my card to make the payment and I was directed into a small field to pitch my tent. There were only two other tents and I had the choice of where to pitch, and so I set up in a corner of the field underneath a tree for extra shelter, facing my door in the direction of the hedgerows for privacy. All seemed to be well and I was quite content and somewhat relieved to be there, at least for a short while.

After unpacking my gear and arranging it all in its normal places within the tent, I took a gentle stroll back to the reception to enquire about the shop. With my stomach rumbling in anticipation of a pasty or even just a bar of chocolate, my worst fears were realised. Due to the pandemic, the shop had been forced to close and wouldn't be open again for the foreseeable future. My heart sank as the site owner explained that the only shop available in the area was the one the two elderly hikers had informed of just a few hours earlier, in Hartland village. I had no choice but to make the three mile round trip along the country lanes if I wanted to get any supplies. The next stop along the coast that provided food of any kind was Clovelly, and that was many miles away. This was a disaster. If I'd have known that the shop was closed, I think I would have pushed on further up the coast and survived the evening on what little food I had left, a Pot Noodle and a Snickers bar, and get into Clovelly for a proper meal as soon as I could the following day. I would have also saved myself ten quid and had a beautiful view over the sea, rather than a bush filled with strident sparrows.

Cursing my poor judgement, I set off on the mile and a half walk along the leafy lanes to Hartland, not even knowing if the store in the village would be open. I was thankful that I'd arrived early enough to the campsite, that I had the option to make the distance before the sun set, and on arrival in Hartland, I was relieved to find a wonderful family-run store, brimming with essentials. I decided to take full advantage of their wares and purchased enough food to last me a couple of long days. Pies, more noodles, chocolate bars and salty snacks, along with four cans of beer. If I was going to be spending the night in a campsite, I was going to make sure I enjoyed myself!

What didn't occur to me while making the purchase, was the fact I would have to carry all of these products back to the tent, and in my haste when setting off on the walk, I'd not even brought a bag. And so, with two flimsy carrier bags, one in each hand, I started the march in reverse. It was tiring to say the least. The food and beer was heavy, and I frequently had to stop to make sure the bags were still intact.

The weight and the paved roads began to take its toll on my legs. I wasn't even half way back to Stoke village, when I felt a severe shooting pain in my left shin, but instead of stopping to rest, I foolishly pushed on, quicker in fact, to get back as soon as possible. That was obviously the wrong thing to do and I would regret that decision in the coming days, but for now, I had one thing on my mind, to get to the tent, eat, drink and have a good nights sleep in a peaceful campsite.

The perfect vision of a quiet, restful nights sleep was shattered the moment I entered the camping field. Even though there were only two tents in the vicinity, and the occupants of the tent closest to me were clearly out for the evening somewhere, the holiday-makers in the other tent had obviously chosen to let their hair down and party for the night, more than making up for any noise my closest neighbours would have made. I'll be honest though, when I first arrived back and shuffled past their tent with my bulging shopping bags, I was greeted by both of them quite amiably. They were both a few years younger than me, a Welsh guy and his girlfriend and they were enjoying a few beverages and a couple of burgers, and the music they were playing, I seem to remember, was very enjoyable. Although this was set to change later in the evening, when they began to listen to a live album recording of a Welsh artist similar to Roy 'Chubby' Brown or Kevin 'Bloody' Wilson, neither of which particularly appeal to my sense of humour. At first, I just smiled. Cracking open a can of beer and scoffing on pastries and chocolate, it was like being at a music festival, and I reminisced about the amazing time I had at Glastonbury in 2003.

After four cans of beer and listening to the same awful tunes and muffled laughter for a couple of hours, it got a little tedious. It was Glastonbury no more, and only now reminiscent of the countless number of annoying neighbours that used to play loud music or had slammed doors shut while I tried to sleep, in the majority of houses that I've lived in in the past. It was time for a festival of my own, and so I put in my earbuds for full control of my aural pleasure. I cannot remember for certain what music I chose to fall asleep to that night, but I have a feeling it was something in complete contrast to what I'd been forced to listen to by the noisy neighbours, something like Level 42 for instance. Embarrassing as that sounds, Mark King's funky basslines certainly do provide an element of external noise-cancelling!

As wonderful and soothing as Mr. King's foot-tapping grooves are (Yes, ok, it *was* Level 42 I fell asleep to!), they are not loud enough to prevent the rumble of an engine waking me in the late evening. Curious to know who my other neighbours were, I paused my tunes and listened for a while, half-expecting boisterous children and a dog barking. I was pleasantly surprised to hear two adult voices exit the car in the silence that now befell the campsite, the rowdy couple obviously having drank too much and retired to bed themselves. They sounded mature and respectful and I doubted I'd have any problems for the rest of the evening, even though it was clear that they too, had had a little too much to drink while they were out.

As I listened intently, I overheard their discussion. They were talking about something I knew quite a lot about, but not wishing to divulge the subject matter, I will just say that the woman seemed to think she was knowledgeable about it, but clearly had no idea...and that frustrated the hell out of me. The guy didn't seem at all interested, but for an hour, the woman continually lectured him with insights I can only imagine she read in a glossy magazine. I'm not quite sure how I managed to get through an hour of that conversation without bursting out of my tent in a Jeremy Kyle rage. People say you should never go to bed angry, and so I have to thank Mr. King once again for his soothing riffs on one of my favourite songs, 'It's Over', for sending me into a peaceful slumber.

SEPTEMBER 14TH

Fully stocked with food, water and battery charge, I headed back to the coast around 9am the following morning. I was a little unprepared for two or three steep ascents before reaching Hartland Point, and so I took an extended break and had a second breakfast on a bench overlooking Shipload Bay.

Today, I was going to Clovelly. It was a village that a good friend of mine had been visiting for several years to celebrate his birthday, and I think he was probably more excited about me visiting the place, than I was. However, I'd promised to see it with my own eyes and so I didn't want to disappoint. Unfortunately, if I'd have known then what I know now, things may have been a little different.

Clovelly is a very secluded village, and if it hadn't have been for two hikers travelling in the opposite direction to me, I would have missed the only turning off the trail for it. They were also wanting to visit and as they approached, they asked me for directions. I told them I was heading there, but that seemed to confuse them, which in turn, confused me. Pointing to the map in their hands, it turned out that I had missed the path by some distance and I was the one heading in the wrong direction, not them. With everyone in agreement, I turned around and walked back along the trail with them, all three of us being forced to chat, which I'm not quite sure they were up for, but felt obliged to do so, as did I. As soon as the turn off was in sight, they were on their way, and I thanked them for saving me an extra few miles on my day, as they scurried off down the cobbled path towards the village centre.

I'm not quite sure what to say about my experience arriving in Clovelly. For those who have been there, they know it is just one, steep cobbled pathway, awkward, whether you are carrying anything on your back or not, and that was quite obvious by the myriad of red-faced tourists, puffing and panting as they climbed the gruelling ascent. It's a beautiful village with whitewashed cottages, and floral decor bordering the main thoroughfare to the harbour, but it's worryingly bumpy, with every step needing utmost attention to prevent a fall. As I descended, each agonising footstep took me closer to sea level and meant I would have to endure the reverse to return to the trail, but once I'd walked a couple of hundred yards, it was obvious I was committed, I might as well continue to the bottom and endure the agony after a pub lunch at the Harbour Restaurant.

It was a busy little quayside and I was amazed by the fact that so many people had taken to walking all this way, just to have to walk back up with the threat of heart attack and heat exhaustion looming over them. For some however, there was a taxi service, which ferried residents of the adjoining hotel to the top of the hill, using a smooth tarmac road, which snaked its way through the woodlands to the west of the village. I was lucky enough to be sitting next to a couple of the hotel guests as I munched on a lovely plate of fish and chips, and they pointed out the guy that drove the taxi. He had only a few runs left in the day before finishing for the afternoon, and as he approached the guests to chat, I jokingly asked (but very seriously pleaded) if he would be willing to take me to the top for a couple of quid. The very lovely people I sat next to directed the drivers gaze to my weighty pack and he sympathetically agreed to spare me the torture of the cobbled climb, and even refused payment. I was so grateful to him and those two hotel guests, it had spared me time and a great deal of effort, and as he whisked me up the hillside in the back of his jeep, I felt an overwhelming sense of goodwill.

The next few miles along what is known as Hobby Drive were pretty tough. Relatively flat and gravelly mostly, but rocky in places and quite arduous. It was a long woodland stretch of trail that was probably quite appealing to day walkers and dog walkers, but for me it was not at all pleasant. To top things off, the pain in my shin had returned and it was becoming an effort with each footstep. I had also forgotten to restock my water supplies, but thinking that I'd come across a natural water source within the wood, I wasn't too worried to begin with. Unfortunately, I failed to find any running water at all. The past few days had been rain-free and quite hot, and I'd drank a lot more than I'd realised.

For the next eight miles I struggled on, chomping on Snickers bars to give me energy boosts, but as the sun began to set, I was in a lot of pain, very thirsty and there was nowhere in sight to camp. Thick gorse bushes along narrow pathways seemed endless and it was becoming worrying, to the point where I even considered cowboy camping on any piece of grass I could find, however small. The pain in my shin increased ten-fold in a matter of minutes as I scaled the overgrown hillsides, and no amount of ibuprofen was going to ease it.

I was lucky to come across a running water source in a little cove and filtered a litre. As the water flowed into my bottle, I looked around the area as a possible camping spot, but noticing lines of seaweed and trash upon the rocks all around me, I knew I was below the high tide line. I had to continue. Another steep climb along a path barely two feet wide didn't fill me with hope, but as I reached the summit of Cockington Cliff, my eyes lit up with the promise of flat, green open land ahead. I limped in agony, the pain being so intense, I actually wondered if I had broken a bone and not just developed a shin splint. Thoughts raced through my head about the mileage that lay ahead and how I was so close to finishing the trail, but now the very real possibility of having to end my journey prematurely was firmly fixed in my mind, and I felt numb. As I pitched my tent in the waning light, my eyes filled with a few tears out of frustration, imagining the worst. It was clear I wouldn't be able to walk the last ninety miles in unbearable pain. If I was to reach Minehead, I would need to take a couple of days break to recover.

SEPTEMBER 15TH

I woke very early the next morning. I'd slept with my legs raised upon my backpack in the hope it would ease some of the pain, and to some extent, it had worked. Gingerly, I collapsed my tent and packed away my gear, then took my first tentative steps on the trail. I was only a mile or so from the town of Westward Ho! and it was thankfully all flat walking, but it was a slow process. I had to stop several times for breaks (I didn't want to push too hard) but I knew it was only a matter of time before the aching in my shin turned into pain once again, and so, as I approached the seawall in the town, I made the decision to search for a bed and breakfast for the following two nights to recover.

There was nothing available in Westward Ho! itself, certainly not for this night, and looking further afield, I realised I was going to have to skip ahead on the trail to the town of Barnstaple, some twenty miles or so along the coast. I was a little gutted, but at least I'd have more chance of crossing that finishing line in Minehead and I wouldn't have to cut the trip short.

I booked a room at a Travelodge for the first night. I'd stayed in one of these places before and found them to be quite agreeable. It was just a matter of getting there and although I could have taken a taxi, I opted for a bus instead. Unfortunately, the bus to Barnstaple ran from Bideford, and as my shin seemed to be holding up at that moment, I decided to take a very slow walk from Westward Ho! to the bus terminal, a few miles away.

I reached Bideford around lunchtime. The bus wasn't due for another hour, having just missed one, and as the rain began to fall, I headed into a pub across the road, where I was welcomed heartily by the landlord with the cheapest pint of Staropramen I'd ever had. This turned into two. Well, at those prices, who wouldn't take advantage? I sat contently watching football on a large screen, occasionally keeping check on the time so as not to miss the next bus and be forced to drink more. Two pints was enough and I stumbled out of the pub with five minutes to spare. The rain had abated and the sun was attempting an appearance from behind some very dark clouds, giving me the perfect opportunity to hide my reddening eyes behind my sunglasses.

I like Travelodges, but they're notoriously difficult to get to if you're not driving a vehicle. I walked down several roads on an industrial estate before realising I'd have to approach the hotel across a roundabout with no footpaths, and through a petrol station forecourt. Despite a couple of close calls with speeding vehicles, I booked in at the reception and relaxed for the rest of the afternoon watching television and filling my stomach with McDonalds from their conveniently situated restaurant just seconds away from the hotel. In the evening I took a long, hot shower and washed a few sweaty items of clothing, but knowing that I'd only have a few more days til I was in another bed and breakfast in Minehead, I wasn't too concerned.

SEPTEMBER 16TH

My second night of recovery would be spent in accommodation completely different to the Travelodge experience, and far more expensive. It was a plush, four star hotel and I was a little worried that my appearance would not meet expectation. Carrying a grubby backpack and wearing muddy shoes, I approached the reception area. The floors were polished white tiles and seemed to glint in the ambient lighting. There was a large bar area to my left with very expensive looking sofas and through elegant wooden doors to my right, the restaurant, clean and shimmering with a myriad of reflective surfaces. As a hiker, I may have been a little out of place as I passed guests in white collars and buffed shoes, but the welcoming lady behind the granite-topped desk was very kind and within a few minutes, I was ascending the classy staircase to my comfortable room.

Barnstaple town centre was just a short walk along the banks of the River Taw and with a few hours on my hands, I thought I'd go for a walk around. I needed a new gas cannister for my stove anyway and so I popped into a local outdoor store. After browsing for fifteen minutes, I exited the store with a new lightweight t-shirt, a small cannister and a brand new head torch. My old Black Diamond torch had a loose connection and I'd thrust a small piece of tin foil between the batteries so they would make the connection needed, and it didn't always work. I chose a Petzl after very little deliberation, as I'd heard so many good reviews about this particular brand. It also had a rechargeable battery, so I wouldn't have to worry about replacing it for new ones any more, always a bonus.

I passed a pub on my way back to the hotel and thought I'd drop in for a bite to eat. It was quite a rough place, but the beer and food were very cheap. I could see why the prices were so low as I was served my burger, it was burnt to a cinder! The few chips that it came with were also over-cooked but were compensated with a tiny amount of lettuce and two squished slices of tomato. As I took my first bite into the burger I felt a crunch, as the crispy edges crumbled into dust in my mouth. It was a very interesting experience, but even though it was not gourmet cuisine, it was actually quite tasty, as I'm sure the many people queuing at the door would agree.

I watched in amazement as the serving staff brought out meal after meal from the smoking kitchen, on highly decorative crockery (The kind of thing you would expect to receive a sunday lunch on...at your grandmothers...in 1975!). It was quite the contrast, eating in that pub and then returning to dine in a four star restaurant later in the evening. From wiping my lips on a square of patterned kitchen roll while listening to Boyzone rumble over the PA system, to dabbing the corners of my mouth with laced napkins in the soothing company of a Brahms concerto, it was one extreme to the other in a matter of hours, but I enjoyed it all equally.

SEPTEMBER 17TH

A delicious breakfast and an extra dent in the wallet as I paid for it, and I was on my way again. Two nights rest had done the trick and I felt at full strength once more. This was it, the final few days' push to MInehead, there was no looking back now, the excitement was almost unbearable. The sun was out, my clothes were clean, I was fully stocked with food and water and I strode along the trail with my heart beating in rhythm with each step. For a few miles, the South West Coast Path was shared with the Tarka Trail along the banks of the River Taw estuary. It was wide, flat and used by cyclists as well as pedestrians, and there were many of each. The tide was low and the many sand banks glistened in the morning sun, it was dazzling at times, enough to make my eyes water.

The trail turned sharply south east as I approached Braunton, and followed the River Caen upon high flood banks. It was a very nice walk into a warm, morning breeze. It was quite reminiscent of the Fen Lands of South Lincolnshire, I thought. (A place dear to my heart and somewhere I'd love to live). Even when the trail turned back north into sand dunes and marram grass, I was so upbeat, I didn't care. The morning had been perfect so far and nothing was going to spoil it.

I got a little startled at one point, as from out of nowhere it seemed, a group of army cadets appeared. They must have been training in the area and as I passed them, I felt eyes piercing into me, probably sniggering about the size and weight of my pack in relation to theirs. 'Let's see you walk 550 miles with that kit on!', I joked silently to myself, but then the truth hit me instantly, their packs were probably twice the weight of mine *and* they'd be able to run the distance. Respect to them and all they do for us.

After skipping through Croyde at some pace, the lengthy peninsula of Baggy Point lay before me. I'd considered cutting across and avoiding it altogether, but the climb up Middleborough Hill looked too much like hard work on a late afternoon, and so I continued on the main coast path. A long, sloping grassy field past Napps Cliff gave me an excellent view of Woolacombe across the bay and a goal to aim for. I was running low on water by this point and considered stocking up somewhere, rather than hoping to find a spring, but there wasn't a shop in sight as I entered the town, just a hoard of people sitting outside the bars along the main roads. I checked the internet for stores in a smaller village, slightly inland, but not far off the coast path, Mortehoe. The road was long and uphill, and I finally arrived at the store late afternoon, only to be disappointed to see a small sign in the window informing me of a closure due to a bereavement, and that it wouldn't be open again until the following day.

As I turned and headed for the connecting footpath to lead me back to the coast, I saw a cosy pub on the brow of the hill. I still had an hour before the sun went down and I knew I needed some liquid inside me. Well, it would have been rude to visit Mortehoe and not give something to the local community, and so I thought a nice crisp five pound note for a beer would do it!

It didn't take me long to find a lovely camp spot in a concealed dip, just before the lighthouse at Bull Point came into view. There were narrow paths through long bracken and it wasn't clear if they had been made by man or beast, but I went for it anyway, and although the evening dampness soaked the bottom of my trousers, it was worth it to find a small, sheltered patch of flat grass right on the coast.

As I began to pitch my tent, confident that nobody would be passing this way at this time of the evening, something caught my eye. It looked remarkably like someone was watching me from the path i'd just come. I'd already passed an odd looking man, acting strangely in the valley before this and wondered if it was him, following me. I'd come to the conclusion he was a photographer though, waiting until the sky turned its familiar red colour at this time of day and thought nothing more of it. I was a little paranoid for quite a while and even put the tent pitching on hold until I could figure what the best course of action would be.

I decided to take a casual walk back through the bracken, leaving my gear where it was and pretending not to see the man watching me, just to see what his reaction would be. After several cautious footsteps in his direction, and noticing that he hadn't moved an inch in the last five minutes, in fact, he hadn't moved an inch in the last year probably, as it turned out to be a long stalk of heather, poking its head from within the bracken fields. And even though I was now aware that it wasn't a person after all, it was still very creepy in the half-light and I still had to look back a couple of times just to make sure. It wasn't until the darkness had swept across the land and I could see it no more, that I finally relaxed and crawled into my sleeping bag for a good nights sleep.

SEPTEMBER 18TH

Today was my birthday. It was the day I'd originally planned to be crossing the finish line in Minehead, but after re-considering, decided that I would enjoy it more spending the day on trail, rather than having to find a bed and breakfast and possibly even drive home. And besides, I wouldn't know how I would be feeling once I'd completed the journey, and if I felt a little depressed about that, it would ruin the day completely. Who wants to be depressed *and* drive for three hours up the M5 on their birthday? I'd make the right decision, albeit forced upon me by injury in the end.

I arrived in Ilfracombe mid-morning and headed off trail to find an eatery of some description. I was happy to stumble upon a small cafe serving fresh coffee and bacon sandwiches. It was just what the doctor ordered and the bacon was cooked just the way I like it, crispy. I could have sat there for hours, watching the world go by, but eventually I forced myself to move on, knowing that the trail would soon enter the Exmoor National Park and I would have some serious climbs to undertake.

The coast between Ilfracombe and Combe Martin was incredibly pretty and I soaked up every last viewpoint in the beautiful morning sun. It had been such a steady walk, that I entered Combe Martin at lunchtime and the tasty bacon sandwiches I'd had a few hours before had been burned off and I was running on a low tank once more. There was only one thing for it, a pub lunch. I entered the Dolphin Inn, conveniently located just a few steps from the trail in the centre of the village and ordered a chilli con carne, a pub favourite of mine, and a meal which I frequently cooked myself at home. Of course, I would always compare them to my own, and this one certainly hit the spot...but obviously not *quite* as tasty as mine!

An hour or so passed before I ventured out into the friday afternoon crowds, a little intoxicated after a couple of strong beers. With the vision of a perfect birthday camping spot in mind, atop a cliff and watching a glorious sunset, I found a store that sold beer and squeezed a four-pack of San Miguel into the top of my pack. It was quite heavy of course, but I knew it would be worth it later in the day.

Exmoor is only a few steps from Combe Martin and the trail began to ascend quite quickly, climbing to the Little Hangman summit less than a mile from the village. I would soon reach the highest point on the coast path, Great Hangman, and have a fantastic view of the surrounding area. It was incredibly windy at the top, but quite invigorating, and I had the peak all to myself.

The wind began to increase in strength as I passed Elwill Bay and the stunning cliffs of the North Exmoor coast. So much so, it was beginning to get a little annoying. At times I would swear I was walking at a ninety degree angle to brace myself against the barrage of gusts, swirling around me from all directions. My pack was so heavy that every blast of wind felt like it was trying to rid me of the weight, throwing me off the trail and into the fencing that bordered the adjacent fields. Not even my trekking pole, thrust sternly against the ground to fortify my stance, could keep me in a linear motion.

It was nearing the end of the day and the elements and terrain were firmly against me. As I began to descend the steep drop into Heddon's Mouth Cleave, grasping at the wire fence to keep me upright, I realised I was heading into a section of uneven ground and it was going to be very difficult to find anywhere suitable to pitch my tent. I crouched low, shielding my raw hands as I consulted the map. The contour lines were tightly packed for many miles to come, meaning steep slopes, certainly not conducive to pitching up. There was one hope, the solitary flat peak of East Cleave. As I'd passed it earlier, the wind had prevented me from looking up and so I didn't even notice it was there. I turned, and the wind fired brutally into my back, thrusting me forward without any effort on my part. On approach to the summit, it looked wiry and overgrown with thorny gorse, but on closer inspection, the very top offered a stunning patch of short, green grass, just large enough to fit my one person tent.

It took me quite a while to pitch up. A tent that normally takes about five minutes to erect, must have taken nearly twenty in the stormy conditions. I had to make sure everything was strapped down, pegged down and zipped up. It was tough, but actually quite a fun challenge. After the final peg went in, securing the last guyline to the ground, I took a walk around the pitch. It looked perfect, and the straps I'd created using my shoelaces were holding just fine. Content in the knowledge that this was going to keep me safe for the evening, I unpacked the rest of my gear, threw on a few extra clothes to keep me warm and cracked open a can of beer. Despite the constant winds throughout the night, I was treated to a stunning sunset, had a great meal and slept soundly. Happy birthday to me!

SEPTEMBER 19TH

It was still rather breezy the following morning, but there was no rain and the views were stunning. I had made the right choice by returning to East Cleave the night before, there was absolutely nowhere to camp for quite a distance. A long stretch of woodland around Woody Bay protected me from the mornings wind and when I finally emerged from the greenery, I was greeted with a calmer feel. A tough road climb past Lee Abbey opened up to a wonderful view of The Valley of Rocks. I'd heard good things about this section and I wasn't disappointed. The path was well maintained, and even though it felt quite exposed in some parts, there was a sense of comfort, with the amazing rock faces above me providing some security.

The path brought me out in Lynton, a picturesque town, high on the hillside. It overlooked the incredible Glen Lyn Gorge and the smaller harbour village of Lynmouth, clearly overshadowed by its bigger sibling, but just as beautiful. Between the harbour and Lynton is the Cliff Railway, the worlds highest and steepest water powered railway, in fact. It wasn't running on the day, but for the sake of a swift but lofty descent through some pretty gardens, I don't think I'd have used it anyway.

I chose to find a cafe and buy myself a full English breakfast. I thought I'd earned it. Jauntily striding down the pretty main street, I happened upon The Old Coach House cafe, where I sat in the window, watching the world go by, and enjoyed a huge plateful of sausage, bacon, eggs and more. It was scrumptious to say the least.

Having such a big meal inside me, I thought it'd be a good idea to use the cafe's toilet before I left. It was situated at the bottom of a tiny alleyway, whose ceiling was so low I had to stoop to prevent bashing my head. It was a dingy cave of a convenience with a solitary chair placed just outside the door, to seat those who waited for the next vacancy. Closing the ageing wooden door behind me, I realised that there was a huge gap between it and the door frame, allowing a full view of the throne to anyone who perched on the chair waiting. I am happy to report that I wasn't disturbed, but I often wonder how many embarrassed faces there must have been in the past. I think I'm going to call Guinness and ask them if there's an entry for the fastest toilet break, I would certainly have been in with a shot of getting my name in their book.

An arduous climb out of Lynmouth to Butter Hill left me a little exhausted after my breakfast. I was also more tired than usual and so, with the weather being so nice I took an hours break by the trig point, sheltered from a cooling breeze by a small building used for telecommunications. I think at one point I actually fell asleep, until an inquisitive terrier woke me with a start as it sniffed my grubby clothes. The owner apologised, but I was thankful it had snapped me out of my slumber, as I would probably have lay there for the rest of the afternoon.

I was less than twenty miles from Minehead now and I had yet another long section of woodland to negotiate, in which, at some stage, I would cross over the border into Somerset. The hike was pretty but unchanging, except for a large area of deforestation, where the trail became suddenly confusing. I followed the logging roads, but I wasn't sure I was on the coast path and my gps placed me in the middle of nowhere. After an enquiry to another hiker, I was assured that I had crossed into Somerset and my spirits were raised.

A further few miles through Culbone wood and I arrived at the quaint St. Beuno's Church, situated in a lush green dell, over a mile from the nearest road. It is said to be the smallest parish church in England, and still used for services to this day. To be honest, I found it a little creepy and didn't stay too long.

Another mile or so of woodland, until I appeared to a host of people sitting outside the Ship Inn in Porlock Weir. I'd hoped to get a quick pint and enjoy the views across Porlock Bay, but not only was every seat outside the pub taken, the walls on the opposite side of the road were also filled to capacity. It *was* a saturday night, after all. A little gutted, I decided to walk along the road and head into the larger village of Porlock itself. It was quite a busy route and with no path, I had to shuffle into the undergrowth as each vehicle passed.

This was going to be my last night on trail and I had Bossington Hill as my camping destination. It stood proudly over the bay and was National Trust land, meaning I shouldn't have any land owner issues with my stay. Standing at 243 metres, it was quite a climb and I'd already hiked nearly twenty miles, but this didn't prevent me from purchasing a few more beers from a small store in Porlock though.

I trudged across muddy fields and puddled gravel paths, even though there had been very little rain within the previous few days. The hill was towering before me but it felt like I was not getting any nearer to my goal. There were a couple of routes to the top and I chose a bridle path from Bossington village and an abrupt climb up Hurlstone Combe. It nearly killed me. After walking twenty three miles, my legs were aching and my heart was thumping hard. I was slightly dehydrated, my mouth being dry and salty and my temples were throbbing across my forehead. I had to stop for five minutes half way, even though the daylight was fast fading. I'm so glad I did, not just to recover from the effort of the climb, but as I sat looking at the ascent I'd just endured, a deer appeared from behind a bush just several feet away from me. We stared at each other for what seemed like eternity, both unflinching. When the beautiful creature decided I was no threat to her, she casually walked away, looking back only once as if to say goodbye and good luck. It was a moment that will stay with me forever.

Suddenly empowered by what had just happened, I made my way to the top of the hill in strides. There were plenty of places to camp, and I nestled behind a gorse bush to enjoy my final evening on the trail.

SEPTEMBER 20TH

It was a beautiful sunday morning and the clouds rolled gently over the distant hills. I was less than five miles from the end of the trail and I was in no rush to get there. Since the 12th of august on that intensely hot afternoon, I had been walking the south west coast of England. Over sand dunes, grassy fields and tarmac roads; across rocky terrain, pebbled beaches and soft muddy estuaries; through woodlands, towns and villages, camping where I could or sleeping in plush accommodation, the journey had been diverse. Eating out of my cooking pot over a stove or sampling the culinary delights of local cuisine in pubs and restaurants, the journey had been an experience. The people I met, places I visited, wildlife I encountered, the journey had been emotional. I'd climbed the height of Mount Everest nearly four times over, walked in excess of six hundred miles, seen the most incredible sunsets and sunrises and felt the wrath of mother nature's storms and wind. I'd been scared, excited, worried and content, sometimes experiencing all four emotions on the same day. There has been nothing in my life that can compare to those forty days and it was all about to come to an end.

I sat under a tree and boiled water for a warm cup of coffee for the very last time, trying to comprehend what the day meant to me. In some respects I was happy that it was all over, in others, I was devastated that I would be returning to 'normal' life very soon. As my mind played tug-of-war with my emotions, I thought about everything I had experienced over the last month or so and tried to weigh it all up. There was the stress of finding places to camp, catching ferries, searching for water and cleaning clothes, to name but a few, but whatever negative I could think of, it was immediately replaced with many positives, and the biggest one of all, was the feeling of freedom.

Never has five miles taken me so long to walk, but never has that distance provided so much anticipation, expectation or most certainly, pride. I'd like to say there was a marching band and several thousand people cheering, on my approach to the trail monument on the promenade at Minehead, but the reality was misty, cold, desolate and lonely. I was lucky to have reached it at the perfect moment to interrupt a couple of morning walkers, and asked if they would kindly take a photo of me. I was grateful that they obliged.

As the couple left me, I realised I was completely alone. I felt a little numb in the morning dampness, the realisation that there was no more coast to walk. I felt lost, unsure of my next movements. There was nowhere else to go, this was the end of the line.

I sauntered along the promenade, dodging each wave that crashed violently against the sea wall, I turned towards the centre of Minehead and for the final time, I left the sea behind.

WITH THANKS:

My mum – For car and worldly possession storage and receiving smelly clothing through the mail

Julia – For pre-hike accommodation and hearty meals

The Woodlands Hotel, Sidmouth

Warwick Guest House, Penzance – For the best breakfast in Cornwall

Noel

The wonderful taxi guy at Clovelly, Devon

The hardy ferryman at Bantham, Devon – For working on a sunday

The beautiful running lady of West Lulworth – For obvious reasons

The person who gave a home to a trekking pole I left next to a bench in Salcombe, Devon

The thru-hikers on Golden Cap for giving me info on diversions

Jon in Budleigh Salterton for including me in his video

Printed in Great Britain
by Amazon